MW00334074

The RD
of IRON

THE ROD OF IRON © copyright 2018 by Wade Fransson.
All rights reserved. No part of this book may be reproduced in any form whatsoever, by photography or xerography or by any other means, by broadcast or transmission, by translation into any kind of language, nor by recording electronically or otherwise without permission in writing from the author, except by a reviewer who may quote brief passages in critical articles or reviews.

Anthem
Words and Music by Alex Harvey, Hugh McKenna Copyright © 1992 Sony/ATV Music Publishing LLC All Rights Reserved – Permission Requested from Sony.
Unless otherwise noted, Scripture quotations are from the Authorized (King James) Version.

Scriptures quotations marked (NIV) are taken from the Holy Bible, New International Version®, NIV®. Copyright © 1973, 1978, 1984, 2011 by Biblica, Inc.™ Used by permission of Zondervan. All rights reserved worldwide. www.zondervan.com. The "NIV" and "New International Version" are trademarks registered in the United States Patent and Trademark Office by Biblica, Inc.™

ISBN 13: 978-1-7324511-1-7
Library of Congress Control Number: 2018907824
Printed in the United States of America
First Printing: 2018

18 17 16 15 14   5 4 3 2 1

Edited by Rebecca Miller
Cover art by Judith Nicols
Cover design by Glen Edelstein
Interior design by Glen Edelstein

SOMETHING
OR OTHER
PUBLISHING

Info@SOOPLLC.com
For bulk orders e-mail: Orders@SOOPLLC.com

To the moon, for reflecting the light. And to my Angel, my personal moon, who pulled me out of an elliptic orbit, and helped me appreciate its true beauty.

CONTENTS

FOREWORD

The Rod of Iron is the third volume of a trilogy in which author Wade Fransson meticulously weaves myriad threads of experience from his rich and unique life into a narrative tapestry. That narrative represents a painfully personalized and almost confessional revelation intended to assist the reader in grasping its details while seeing them in relation to his spiritual quest, a preoccupation initially imposed upon him by his driven evangelical father but which soon becomes Fransson's own personal passion.

For most Christians, the wealth of prophesies found both in The Old and New Testaments are encountered during church services, but rarely play a central role in their lives. For Fransson, as with many other followers of the Worldwide Church of God, they did, which distinguished them among Christians. Their theological interests focused specifically on the Bible's rich prophetic writings and heritage, especially those referring to the return of Christ. In the case of author Fransson, however, this compelling, life-long pursuit extends to a willingness to pursue his investigation of biblical prophecy outside the context and confines of the delivered explanations of its founder, Herbert W. Armstrong. His newfound openness to the discoveries of modern science and expanding into diverse religious inputs has yielded exceptional results.

In his earlier years, as Fransson was confronting those vicissitudes of life with which we can all identify, one observing him might have considered his intense preoccupation with God and the Bible as a kind of magnificent obsession as it were, as a passion abstracted from a compartmentalized or disconnected personality. This biblical interest continued to dominate his life while serving as a leader and minister with the Worldwide Church of God, during which he gained exposure to diverse populations of the world with their varied languages and cultures. It was during this time that more thought and serious concern was being directed towards aligning his personal life, to bring it in sync with his broader moral beliefs, vs. the narrow, literal, rigid interpretation of the Worldwide Church of God. When that church split over the issues that Fransson was also struggling with, and facing the growing economic demands of providing for a family, Fransson left the ministry and entered the for-profit sector. Surprisingly, he enjoyed a skyrocketing trajectory which took him to lofty administrative levels within that increasingly materialistic world.

It was as a conscionable individual functioning within that morally compromised corporate work environment that Fransson found himself going through what might be tagged a serendipitous heart-mind dialectic process which involved both the angst that comes from having gained a growing awareness of the mistakes he had made in life, which included a failed marriage, a work environment replete with pressures for moral compromise, while experiencing a quantum leap in his growing knowledge of the astounding prophecies found in the Bible concerning the return of Christ.

During this period of intense soul-searching and reflection his heart was reawakened by romance. He met and fell in love with a lovely soul named Angela. As it turned out, meeting, courting, and falling in love with this lovely individual also carried with it the synchronous exposure to and involvement with a here-to-fore unknown, at least to him, Faith Community whose Writings claimed to have solved the riddle regarding the all-consuming quest of many scripture-based Christians—the return of the Messiah. The Bahá'ís presented entirely unexpected answers to the questions Fransson had been pursuing over his entire adult life. And moreover, he found that the scriptures and traditions of all existing religions not only expressed a yearning for that same spiritual fulfillment, rebirth, and certainty, but that they could be reconciled with Fransson's knowledge of the Bible.

He has elsewhere stated that his process of accompanying Angela on her study of Bahá'í writings was reminiscent of how in the 1920's the beliefs adopted by Worldwide Church of God founder Armstrong's wife, Loma, forced him to conclude that his wife's "religious fanaticism" was supported by scripture. Fransson's attraction to Angela, who would become his wife, forced him to similarly evaluate the Bahá'í Faith's stupendous claim to be a universal religion whose Revealed Word addresses and fulfills the messianic expectations not only of Christianity but all religious traditions and beliefs systems, with a mission and the promise to unite them all.

In the midst of the past century a charismatic priest, Archbishop of the Roman Catholic Church, Father Fulton J. Sheen authored a book entitled *The Greatest Story Ever Told.* In it he makes the astounding claim that among all religious figures Jesus the Christ is unique, and gives his rationale as to why he believed this to be so, and that the appearance and life of Christ therefore indeed represented the greatest story known to mankind. Obviously, those of other faith traditions would take exception to Bishop Sheen's assertion, with some denying Christ's uniqueness altogether. Few, however, have taken the time or applied the scholarly rigor necessary as Fransson has done to fully explore this magnificent claim, let alone attempt to go beyond it to address the even larger context of reconciling those same prophetic expectations found in other religious traditions.

I can relate to Mr. Fransson's spiritual journey for a different reason, as my father traveled the same pathway. Beginning in 1929, when two of his closest friends had become members of the Bahá'í Faith, he, as a conscionable Christian, wanted to get them back on the right track. Like Fransson, armed with biblical scriptures as a standard, he began what eventually turned out to be a nineteen-year investigation into the Bahá'í Writings all measured against the Bible as the ultimate criterion. He left no scriptural rock unturned. And it was after that long and initially exhausting but eventually exciting, fulfilling, and passionate investigation of both biblical prophecies and the Bahá'í Writings that he experienced an incredible epiphany that changed his life, a transformation that gave new meaning to it, and direction.

So, it was through reading about Fransson's spiritual journey that I experienced in the words of baseball manager, Yogi Bera, a man known for his colorful metaphor, "déjà vu all over again!" I invite you to take this journey with him as I have. I guarantee that as you read his account of wrestling with these profound scriptural, religious and spiritual questions your mind will be challenged, stretched and informed and your heart and spirit warmed and filled with gratitude and affection.

—*Dr. Donald T. Streets,*
Author and Educator

PREFACE

The original rush of inspiration for the manuscript which led to this trilogy was fueled by two scientific discoveries I learned about in 2009.

First a National Public Radio interview with astronomer Edo Berger of the Harvard Smithsonian Center for Astrophysics caught my ear. Berger was discussing the discovery of the oldest object ever recorded—gamma radiation related to the thirteen-billion-year-old death of a star. Just six hundred million years after the big bang. Berger explained the significance of the find in terms of a forty-five-year-old man discovering, for the first time, a picture of himself at age two.[1]

Then an article called "Quantum Afterlife" by Charles Q. Choi in the February 2009 edition of *Scientific American* caught my eye. Choi discusses quantum entanglement—a phenomenon that allows particles to affect each other across distances up to 144 kilometers. His article explains that particle "memories" of entanglement can survive the destruction of the particle, comparing the effect to the novel *Wuthering Heights*, in which Catherine communicates to Heathcliff beyond the grave.[2]

What caught my fancy was how scientists describe their findings using metaphors of birth and death, and our relationship to them. These anthropomorphic analogies strike resonant chords with the humanity at our core of being. We have a deep, strong, abiding desire to know who we are, where

1 David A. Aguilar and Christine Pulliam, "Farthest Known Object: New Gamma-Ray Burst Smashes Cosmic Distance Record," Harvard-Smithsonian Center for Astrophysics, April 28, 2009, https://www.cfa.harvard.edu/news/2009-11.
2 Charles Q. Choi, "Quantum Entanglement Benefits Exist after Links Are Broken," Scientific American, February 1, 2009, https://www.scientificamerican.com/article/quantum-entanglement/.

we came from, and where we are going. A prolific Christian apologist, Ravi Zacharias, believes that any coherent worldview must satisfactorily answer four questions: those regarding origin, meaning of life, morality, and destiny.[3]

Where do we come from? Why are we here? Where are we going? Does what I do matter?

These questions both fascinate and haunt humankind. As we grow ever more sophisticated as a species, we devote ever more resources to answering these mysteries. Whether through supercomputers, space exploration, underground particle accelerators, or just plain old philosophy, we expend enormous amounts of time and energy in pursuit of answers to these simple yet profound questions. These questions call out the natural tension between religion and science, in which religion claims God created man in His image, while science generally claims it happened the other way around.

The history of human evolution is impossible to separate from religion. Beliefs about God and His relationship to us are an integrated focal point of our development. This is clear from whatever type of history we can trace back to whichever creatures can be called human, even if the religiously inclined and the scientifically inclined interpret this fact differently.

Religious creation stories are viewed by scientists as primitive myths through which humans create god. When religion accepts these stories, they often dismiss creation stories outside their authorized texts as pagan corruptions. This volume presents an alternate viewpoint.

A unique feature of these creation stories is an extrapolation extending from the beginning of time right on through to the "end of the world." The manifestation of the universe as visible from earth, the "heavens," is interpreted and used to explain, record, and project epic stories that, while fantastic in nature, have universal appeal to those who seek to understand the universe and our place in it. This includes the zodiac, ancient Egyptian sky charts, and various lunar and solar calendars, including the Mayan calendar that caught the popular imagination in recent years as it famously approached its 2012 ending.

The popularity of such topics indicates that while our Western societies are secularized, interest in biblical end-time prophecy scenarios shows no sign of dying out, at least in the US. Still, those in positions of thought leadership today ride a wave of secular incredulity and skepticism of anything that might be called divine. But this began relatively recently in human history, and even within an overall flow toward secularism, its advocates and proponents resort to religious concepts to express their materialism.

---

3 Bill Pratt, "How Should We Analyze a Worldview?," Tough Questions Answered (blog), June 8, 2012, http://www. toughquestionsanswered.org/2012/06/08/how-should-we-analyze-a-worldview/.

This brings us back to the inputs with which I opened this preface, by those who push the boundaries of what is commonly known as science. These highly intelligent, massively educated minds use the most advanced research projects ever devised to explore the concepts of origins and the events associated with Genesis, as our most ancient ancestors, in their own way, did. They even use terminology such as "the search for the God particle" to describe what they are doing.

Whether in the form of pyramids in Egypt, inexplicable rocks in the field at Stonehenge, Mayan ruins, ancient Scripture, astrology, or legend, the evidence of our search for meaning, and for God in the heavens is overwhelming and indisputable. In 2011, for example, as I was finally completing the manuscript of *The People of the Sign*, I was forwarded a fascinating article, on the most ancient temple ever found, at Göbekli Tepe.[4] What most captured my imagination was the evidence of circumambulation, an emulation of the movement of the particles and heavenly bodies that make up our universe.

Though our stories are unique, they are, like particles, entangled. What we find at the micro, the personal level of humanity—stories of human accomplishment and failure, of success and suffering, enlightenment and hard knocks—are fractal patterns of the macrolevel stories of family, tribe, nation, race, and species.

At the heart of my story is a lifelong attempt to reach for the stars, while being careful to have my feet firmly planted on the foundation of the writings accepted by those who honor Abraham, Moses, and Jesus. My hope is that my experience will support your self-discovery or spiritual awakening in reviewing the ultimate questions against the background of your own quest to find balance. And if the ups and downs of my life provide you with the encouragement needed to take your own next leap of faith, then it will all have been worthwhile.

---

4 Charles C. Mann, "The Birth of Religion," National Geographic, June 2011, 34-59.

(Just Like) Starting Over

You can add up the parts but you won't have the sum
You can strike up the march, there is no drum
Every heart, every heart to love will come
but like a refugee.

Ring the bells that still can ring. Forget your perfect offering
There is a crack in everything. That's how the light gets in.
"*ANTHEM*"—BY LEONARD COHEN

If you were born before 570 BC, you would have lived your life believing the earth was flat. The revelation that it is spherical is attributed to Pythagoras, and Greek scholars accepted this as fact from around 500 BC. This is not to say everyone since then knew this fact or believed it. Rumor has it some still don't. Depending on when and where you were born, you also believed the sun revolved around the earth. The reverse was proposed as early as 300 BC, but that didn't stop the Roman Catholic Church, two thousand years later, from persecuting Galileo for proclaiming this fact.

In more recent times, Newton taught that time and space were an absolute framework, a stage on which our lives played out. You could know the location, past and future, of anything based on a single snapshot of its location and motion. Since Einstein, those who care about such things know that the space-time continuum is curved by the bodies that roll around in it. In this conclusion to the trilogy that began with *The People of the Sign* we'll cover this ground, curved or not, in the light of an even bigger misconception.

Many of those in so-called enlightened countries today believe that there is no God and many who do believe in God view Him as very detached from current world events. My own lifetime search led to the conclusion that these perspectives amount to a "flat-earth" delusion that has much of humanity looking for its edge, with the answers they seek always just out of reach.

AND I LOVE HER

Before we enter any of the bubbles, curvatures, or wormholes that warp the space-time continuum in the direction of divine creation (we will get to them in due time), it's important to consider the specific heavenly body that for most of my life guided my soul on its journey—the moon. More recently, an angel named Angela had unintentionally pulled me gently, willingly, and irresistibly, like the tide, in her direction. After I declared her, in a poem, to be my moon she had finally accepted that my love was true and opened her heart to me.[1]

As I responded to Angela's lead, our relationship grew stronger. Picking a wedding date was a good example of how this worked. She wanted a year to plan and prepare, which was far longer than I had hoped for. But I agreed, and then looked up which spring and summer nights featured a full moon while she researched locations with an ocean view.

Angela found a turn-of-the-century luxury hotel called La Valencia, situated in La Jolla, just north of San Diego. This area, just to the south of where we lived, is known for its perfect climate and was a perfect choice to begin our life together. Anything seems possible when the needle hovers between sixty and eighty degrees all year. I was instantly sold on this magical town with its fantasy climate, where it seemed everything goes, it all works out, and nobody gets hurt.

When we toured La Valencia we saw that it offered an outdoor lawn area overlooking the ocean, just a hundred or so yards away. A park was just across the street at the base of the hill, between us and the water. It featured the Monterey cypress reputed to have provided Dr. Seuss, a long-time resident of the area, inspiration for the Truffula tree in his book *The Lorax*. After checking out the restaurant and dance area, Angela was sold as well. They had an opening on March 31, 2007, a date which coincided with a full moon.

During what to me seemed the eternity of our engagement, I, the tide, continued to follow Angela's lead. This very wise decision helped us grow

1 The poem "The Moon" is included as Appendix 1 .

closer, month by month, planning each and every aspect of the wedding together. There were lots of romantic moments as we traveled back to La Jolla to taste test the menu for the wedding, choose our cake at a local bakery, and prequalify local attractions to recommend to our guests. Even decisions for which I normally had neither patience nor interest, such as the design of invitations, choosing colors and flowers, and the million and one other items eating up my time and wallet, became wonderful opportunities to spend time with her.

Angela is from Wisconsin and moved to sunny Southern California after graduating from the University of Wisconsin–Madison. We met while I was vice president of strategic planning for Countrywide Financial Corporation. One of my responsibilities was location strategy, and I had studied the demographics of Madison, Wisconsin's capital, which always scored high in "quality of life." I kidded her about a quote that I came across labeling Dane County "seventy square miles surrounded by reality." Angela fails to see the humor in this quote, which is that Madison, in Dane County, is as close as the Midwest gets to Disneyland.

My first visit to Dane County was certainly magical. On a gorgeously sunny summer day in 2006, at UW–Madison's Student Union, overlooking Lake Mendota, I asked my future in-laws for their daughter's hand. The pleasant yet nervous experience of this encounter was tainted, however, by the trepidation at having Angela's parents meet mine.

One of the gifts bestowed on me by my father was the introduction to the Worldwide Church of God (WCG), a unique and very zealous religious group that shaped my thinking about God and everything else. The heavenly moon had guided my soul, for example, in that it was the celestial mechanism that established the Hebrew calendar. This went way beyond keeping time. It was the prophetic framework for humankind, which is human history written in advance. This perspective was immeasurably valuable to me, but it did come with some baggage.

For decades I labored under the delusion that the creation of a zodiac, for example, through astronomic observations was a Satan-inspired substitute for God, designed to entrap and enslave us. Satanic deception lurked around every corner, and the collective knowledge and wisdom of humanity was full of darkness stemming from separation from God. The Bible actually indicates the opposite, acknowledging the zodiac and indicating there is some importance to it. The quote below is from an article that draws a conclusion similar to my prior position:

The Bible also teaches that God arranged the stars into recognizable groups that we call constellations. The Bible mentions three of these: Orion, the Bear (Ursa Major), and "the crooked serpent" (most likely Draco) in Job 9:9; 26:13; 38:31-32; and Amos 5:8. The same passages also reference the star group Pleiades (the Seven Stars). God is the One Who "fastens the bands" of these constellations; He is the One who brings them forth, "each in its season." In Job 38:32, God also points to the "Mazzaroth," usually translated "constellations." This is thought by many to be a reference to the twelve constellations of the zodiac.[2]

The article goes on to state that the Bible does not infer any hidden meaning in these verses. I'll come back to this shortly but in the meantime, knowing the above about the Bible, and visiting Stonehenge, the Great Pyramids of Egypt, and the spiritual red-rock area of southeastern India called Tiruvannemalai, softened my perspective.[3]

Having a soul mate on my spiritual search opened new vistas, as I began to see all efforts to explain our universe as divinely inspired inklings that result from looking for light in darkness. There were many remnants from humanity's primordial search for meaning, which revealed that from the time our species could ask questions we were looking for God in the heavens. Modern astrophysics is just the latest evolution of this quest.

In 2006, where we pick up this story, I was increasingly trying to integrate these old and new approaches into a coherent worldview. It hadn't crystalized yet, but I was on the verge of a breakthrough, just tantalizingly outside my reach.

DIG IT

Creation physics and quantum theory provided important perspectives, but for me the Genesis story, as presented in the Bible, held the key. In its opening verses God invites us to look to the heavens He created to understand our destiny—with lights in the sky forming the heavenly calendars of a divine clock, with inherent prophetic and practical seasons and signs, which would physically and spiritually light our way.

2 "What Does the Bible Say about Astrology or the Zodiac? Is Astrology Something a Christian Should Study?," Got Questions, accessed June 26, 2018, https://www.gotquestions.org/astrology-Bible.html.

3 This book is the conclusion of a trilogy that began in The People of the Sign. My initiation into the WCG, my time in its college and ministry, and much more is covered in that volume. My experiences in Egypt, India, and much more are covered in the second volume, The Hardness of the Heart. While this third volume is intended to stand on its own, you may wish to put it down and start at the beginning. Or not ... your search is your own.

My quest was the inverse of that of Copernicus and Galileo, who had used observations to dispel the Middle Ages darkness imposed by the rigid authority of the Roman Catholic Church. The bankruptcy of the Catholic Church's claim of infallibility, and of organized religion in general, has since led many educated people to all but abandon belief in God. Its pervasive power to exterminate anyone who challenged its role as the source of revealed truth has today been usurped by the materialism which later undermined the power of the church. This crushing materialism extinguishes the illumination offered in God's Word. But then and now prophetic promises made by God are a candle burning brightly in darkness if they are read and understood.

These convictions about the Bible had arrived early in my life, when the WCG convinced my father that God was alive, well, and active on the world scene. Though my father disappointed me, God never did. My heavenly Father's intervention in my very difficult life encouraged my devotion to Him, and the challenges He helped me overcome fueled my commitment to seek out the answers to the questions these challenges brought to the forefront.

An early catalyst in my search came when I had traveled, as a young college student, to Israel to participate in the City of David archaeological exhibition. There I peered not up at the heavens but down—into a hole in the ground. Experts declared this particular hole, at Jericho, to be a prehistoric settlement in which humans had begun exploring community life. At the time I was told this was one of the oldest inhabited cities in the world, with the first protective wall and the oldest stone tower. Archaeologists dated the first settlement of Jericho to be eleven thousand years old, one of the cradles of civilization. This challenged my prior conception that all human activity had begun six thousand years ago with Adam and Eve's creation.[4]

Ever since that visit to Israel I had been trying to connect the logical dots between the historical record of humanity's experience and the record of God's revelation, laid down across time by scribes and prophets in the Bible. The challenge, of course, is that the latter is filled with that which the rational call irrational, as typified by the mythological nature of the creation story in its opening pages, the virgin birth of the Savior at its center, and the fantastic visions in the book of Revelation with which it concludes.

And yet, since the events of the 9/11 attacks on the World Trade Center, and the unfolding chaos in the Middle East unleashed by the forces of Islam,

---

4 The WCG taught the "gap theory," which explains the apparent discrepancy between what the fossil record reveals and the account in Genesis 1:2 via translating the word "was" (in "the earth was without form, and void") as "became." An untold amount of time transpired between "the beginning" in Genesis 1:1 and the re-creation/renewal referenced in Psalms and elsewhere. The belief that the Adam and Eve story is largely literal and occurred only six thousand years ago was a different kind of problem. This was the one which preoccupied me.

each and every story in the Bible, and the historical, symbolic, and spiritual elements in them, seemed to have increasing relevance to the events that I saw occurring around me. One brief episode in the epic saga that unfolds across the Bible's sixty-six books is a memorable story in the opening chapters of Genesis. It's the one often referred to as the Tower of Babel, where God supernaturally stops humans from building a tower to heaven. This introduces the concept of what will later become Babylon, and eventually, in end-time prophecy, Babylon the Great. According to the biblical story, the human species was united in a quest to transcend their station on earth. God acknowledged the power of their unity by stating: "Now nothing will be restrained from them, which they have imagined to do." God didn't want this, so He confused their language, destroying their unity, and they scattered across the earth.[5]

God had limited the advancement of the species He created in His image, which prematurely sought to ascend to His throne. But He had created us with that capacity to advance, so why didn't He want us to use it? Angela's spiritual search resurrected my interest in this question.

OCTOPUS'S GARDEN

After arriving in Los Angeles and finding the Los Angeles Catholic community less than embracing, Angela had decided to abandon her Catholic upbringing in favor of a more spiritually satisfying home. In a Yoga teacher's training course, a fellow seeker named Paith had introduced her to the Bahá'í community, and I had attended several local Bahá'í events with her. These included in-home discussion groups and community concerts by local Bahá'í artists at their Los Angeles Center.

At one of these concerts a young man named Devon Gundry performed his folk rendition of a Bahá'í prayer titled "Words for Waking." The way he sang "I give praise to Thee, O my God, that Thou hast awakened me out of my sleep," hit me like an arrow through the heart. The hand of God seemed to be gently but firmly shaking me awake. At about the same time I attended a Bahá'í presentation with Angela and learned about an important figure in the Bahá'í Faith called the Báb. This young Iranian had, in 1844, declared himself to be "the Gate of God."

The Báb came to unite humankind, announcing that there should be a universal language. Knowing that the Hebrew word for God is *El* I mentally read his title—Gate of God—as Báb El. This brought the Tower of Babel to

---

5 Genesis 11 – all Bible quotes are from the King James Version, unless otherwise noted.

mind. That and the date of his declaration, 1844, a date many once believed to hold enormous prophetic significance, was enough to pique my curiosity and keep me interested in this unusual religion Angela had stumbled upon.

This interest had made it easier to be sincere in my desire to accompany Angela on her spiritual quest rather than laboring under the wrongheaded idea that it was my responsibility to be her guide while pursuing my own. And accompanying Angela on her search made it possible for me to attain balance on the spiritual-material tightrope I seemed to always be walking. I could let my own incessant spiritual search take a comfortable back seat while I threw myself wholeheartedly into my corporate career.

My first year as vice president for strategic planning at Countrywide had gone well. I had received the 2004 Rookie of the Year award and worked on increasingly complex problems, affecting large budgets—in the hundreds of millions of dollars. Now I was focused on helping the company double in size, from thirty to sixty thousand employees.

One reason for my initial corporate success was my ability to seek out and understand the so-called "big picture." And at Countrywide, my strategic planning role brought me into contact with the internal community of experts that were developing the overall strategy of the company, across all its divisions. I was also continuing work on the Master of Business Administration degree I had started in my previous position at the accounting and consulting firm Deloitte and Touche. Since I had been dealing with all aspects of business management and administration on a daily basis for the last seven years, it was easy for me to relate to the key concepts from classes and my reading.

With my studies supporting my career in this manner, I was able to deliver high quality work at my day job, and the kind of projects I was working on at Countrywide made excellent case studies and papers. This created a positive feedback loop of success at work and a 4.0 grade-point average in my MBA program. Looking at the business objectively, from the vantage point of my experience and my studies, I gained a unique perspective on the challenges facing Countrywide and was able to make useful recommendations on how to overcome them.

But success led to a reinflation of my ego and my confidence in what I felt I was contributing to the company. This in turn led to challenges in my relationships with others in an all-too-familiar cycle of success, ego growth, then failure. In spite of these challenges, the powers that be at Countrywide were impressed enough with the results that I was given additional responsibilities and promoted to first vice president, one step away from the coveted role of senior vice president. I was on the verge of being able to make a real impact on company performance.

Unfortunately, as I gained access to a higher-level perspective, I began to see something disturbing.

DEVIL IN HER HEART

It started with personal observations about the CEO of Countrywide, Angelo Mozilo. I had the opportunity to ride up and down in the elevator with him on several occasions, and even in those brief interactions it was impossible not to notice that while I certainly struggled to control my ego, he seemed to give his full reign. He openly used ugly language, proclaiming that he would make people pay for daring to cross him, and it did not seem to bother him in the slightest that both his language and his approach were offensive to others.

But that was just the tip of the iceberg.

It didn't matter that he was worth hundreds of millions; he was on a quest to secure and protect his status as a billionaire, and he was not opposed to using all the means available to him at his level of power and wealth to obtain that goal. He had prescheduled massive, ongoing divestitures —weekly sales of stock valued in the millions of dollars. A *New York Times* article from 2007 reveals that "Mr. Mozilo has sold shares through arranged schedules since 2004. But the pace of his sales, which have generated $300 million in gains for him since 2005, began to increase in October 2006 when he put a new program in place."[6]

The pyramid structure I had struggled with at Deloitte, which was used by many of the large companies to whom I provided strategic consulting services during my tenure there, was also in evidence here. These experiences, my course work toward my MBA, and what I was seeing at Countrywide all cemented my conclusions about the system of capitalist corporations in America and globally.

In *The Hardness of the Heart* I compared these corporations to dinosaurs—gargantuan creations that have to consume voraciously to survive and thrive. These corporations exist for the purpose of creating profits, which they do with a cold-blooded focus on the bottom line. The legal structure of a corporation empowers it to act this way while protecting its creators and owners from liabilities generated by their activities.

The more I personally became involved in this fast-growing carnivore known as Countrywide, with its vision/mission expanding from "Making

---

6 Gretchen Morgenson, "Stock Sales by Chief of Lender Questioned, " New York Times, October 11, 2007, http://www.nytimes.com/2007/10/11/business/11land.html.

Home Ownership Affordable" to "Enabling the American Dream," the clearer the full impact of this dinosaur-like behavior became. As this ravenous creature doubled in size, it extended its reach into new businesses. This in turn enhanced its position in the food chain, as it solidified its dominance of the territories it had already conquered.

One of my responsibilities was to provide location strategy for optimal workforce growth. My team researched areas of the country offering the lowest possible cost model, including wages, energy, real estate and facility costs, and taxes. We worked in concert with the workforce planning team in Human Resources. This brought to light how low-wage employees at the bottom of the pyramid enable the aggregation of wealth for the corporation. This wealth can then be siphoned off the top by the owner or operators of the entity.

The full global scale of the economic danger created by turbocharging the criminal inflation of the US real estate bubble was not yet known to the public. Still, at risk of getting just a bit ahead of the story, I can't resist referencing the classic sound bite created by journalist Matt Taibbi, who, in a now-famous series of articles in *Rolling Stone*, explained what happened during this era. Goldman Sachs, one of Countrywide's business partners, he wrote, was a "great vampire squid wrapped around the face of humanity, relentlessly jamming its blood funnel into anything that smells like money."[7]

One of the new businesses Mozilo established was Countrywide Bank. Countrywide Bank enabled Countrywide to create large multiples of debt for every dollar taken in deposits. This rapidly expanded Countrywide's ability to extend credit, enabling it to avoid the expense and bureaucracy of establishing relationships and fee structures with third parties. It dramatically accelerated the growth in size and power of this already large and powerful company.

By bringing more of these critical functions in-house, Countrywide extended its reach, stabilized its cash flow, and diversified its risk portfolio. Countrywide was also able to keep prying eyes out of its business model, making it easier for them to inflate their own market capitalization by controlling the flow of information related to the performance of various components of its increasingly complex operations. The way in which Countrywide did this, and why it mattered, is fascinating, especially to those of us who enjoy watching action movies that feature train wrecks happening in slow motion.

---

7 Matt Taibbi, "The Great American Bubble Machine," Rolling Stone, April 5, 2010, https://www.rollingstone.com/politics/news/the-great-american-bubble-machine-20100405.

DEAR PRUDENCE

Countrywide Bank exploited a loophole in a regulation intended to ensure that a bank has the requisite infrastructure in place at each branch to protect the deposits of its customers.

By ingeniously installing a FedEx drop-off at their new "bank" locations, they allowed customers to make deposits which were not considered deposits. Countrywide Bank thereby avoided the bulk of the real estate, staffing, and security investments normal at bank branches. This allowed a lightning fast rollout of Countrywide Bank branches nationally, and a higher than normal rate of return on CDs offered by the bank. Deposits rolled in like money from a busload of drunken Vegas gamblers, and Countrywide added this rocket fuel to its already turbocharged contribution to the rapidly increasing inflation rate of the real estate bubble.

This blitzkrieg approach to rolling out national bank branches enabled Countrywide to instantly compete effectively with much larger, more established banks. The capital markets ate it up, and Countrywide stock soared. A growing market capitalization brought huge profits to its officers and owners, without impacting the cash it needed to continue expanding. The vast increase in Countrywide assets was deployed and reinvested in a variety of ways. One of these investments was the purchase of billions of dollars of loans originated through companies such as Goldman Sachs, JPMorgan Chase, and others. These purchases were accomplished by Countrywide Wholesale Lending.

The Hardness of the Heart discusses the disaster that was Enron, an energy trading company that successfully deployed arbitrage and energy blackmail to, among other things, create power surges which brought down the electricity grid in California. Having brought California to its knees, energy could be sold back to their victim at hostage prices. Countrywide was not far behind Enron in creative capitalism.

Mozilo installed a trading floor with two hundred people working in the mortgage securitization area, creating mortgage-backed securities, in which Countrywide stripped all the risk out of the mortgages it originated and purchased, and then packaged them up for sale. The ratings agencies were in on the game, applying misleading labels on this toxic sludge so that it could be sold off at enormous profit to unsuspecting and foolish people all around the planet. Countrywide became "the house," in Vegas terminology.

They controlled so many pieces of the legalized gambling on mortgages that they could make money, hand over fist, on multiple steps in the process. And they were so dominant that they could ensure future profits from all the suckers unfortunate enough to be called "customers" by Countrywide. Some Countrywide customers were now gambling at tables set up by Countrywide, even as bets were being placed against the dubious ability of other customers to make payments on the mortgages Countrywide had sold them against real estate at prices which Countrywide not only knew to be inflated but was complicit in inflating.

Much of this history is known, and some of it is documented in the excellent docudrama *The Big Short*, released in 2015. And yet a major component of Countrywide's business model was not mentioned in the movie.

Whoever owns the servicing rights on a mortgage has the right to collect mortgage payments and manage the collection and payment of taxes and insurance premiums in escrow. This naturally includes the right to collect fees for these services. In the end Countrywide owned the servicing rights on 1.3 trillion dollars' worth of mortgages.

Yes, that's trillion with a "*t*".

Now—hypothetically, of course—what do you suppose would happen if the economy were to sputter and falter? Or what might happen if, heaven forbid, the real estate bubble were to, say, burst, taking down the economy in the process? It's pretty obvious that homeowners would have difficulty keeping up with their mortgage payments on their overpriced homes, bringing the house of cards crashing to the floor. Conventional wisdom, even among the optimistic traders, was that this would cause Countrywide to implode.

This is one reason traders were shorting Countrywide stock, which means placing bets against it. Others did so based on Mozilo's personal sales of Countrywide stock. And certainly, the business prospects of many segments of the Countrywide model would be seriously impacted, as mortgage origination and the securitization of mortgages came to a virtual standstill. But the business risk that the market for real estate mortgage risk would collapse was brilliantly mitigated by the unheard-of scale of the then low-margin loan administration business they had retained. In any imaginable scenario, however catastrophic, Countrywide would be far from the hardest hit.

The biggest losers would be the owners and insurers of the underlying real estate and the risk it generated, the mortgage-backed securities, which Countrywide, after making obscene amounts of money creating and trading them, had unloaded on investors. These toxic investments became known as weapons of mass financial destruction because of what would happen when the bubble stopped expanding. They would cause the bubble to burst spectacularly, bringing down many other large companies along with them.

Countrywide was well aware that this would likely happen and had created and deployed a major mitigation strategy to protect itself.

This brings us back to the enormous scale of this bet of 1.3 trillion dollars' worth of servicing rights. I had initially wondered why Countrywide held on to the boring, low-margin servicing rights. I later realized Countrywide wanted these rights exactly because the bubble they helped create was destined to burst.

In an economic meltdown these would be a surprisingly resilient source of lean protein. This was not only Countrywide's survival bunker, but the company stood to make a fortune on the increasing fees that would be generated by millions of borrowers becoming late and then delinquent. Even as the owners of the securities lost everything, the owner of the servicing rights would show increased profits. This is because the fees which mortgage servicers can charge delinquent homeowners are much more lucrative than the standard servicing fees.

Mozilo had blatant disregard for how his actions impacted those who were being defrauded by the system of systems, of which Countrywide was now a significant part. And that included all his employees. He brought to mind Big Jim in Bob Dylan's song "Lily, Rosemary, and the Jack of Hearts," who owned the town's only diamond mine and who "took whatever he wanted to and he laid it all to waste." In any imaginable scenario, Countrywide would likely thrive and grow, while feeding off the carcasses of their devastated customers and competitors, like the colony of maggots feeding on a dead chicken carcass I once had come across during a college summer program in France.[8]

Not surprisingly, one of the most rapidly growing Countrywide units, in terms of employee count, was the loan administration division. I was tasked to assist with negotiations for government incentives for the placement of a new Countrywide campus, with facilities large enough to house ten thousand employees, dedicated to administering this portfolio of service rights. The idea being championed by the head of Loan Administration was to build this complex in Las Vegas, Nevada.

You can't make this stuff up.

I won't go into the reasons for this proposal, but the output of my location strategy work, to put it mildly, did not support it. As I raised various issues with upper management I was instructed to doctor the results so that Vegas might appear more attractive.

There is probably no better metaphor for American-style free market capitalism than the excesses of Sin City.

---

8 As described in The People of the Sign.

EVERY LITTLE THING

As the magnitude of Countrywide's audacity was becoming clear, the magnitude of planning a perfect wedding was becoming obvious as well. The shattering outcome of my previous marriage had taught me not to minimize the importance of these expensive and time-consuming rituals. I continued my faithful efforts to assist Angela in her methodical use of every minute of our one-year engagement to ensure our wedding day was magical. Unfortunately, in Southern California, home of Disneyland, creating magic is very, very expensive.

I felt I needed to continue as a cog in the world of corporate business in order to finance the upcoming wedding and beyond. And this would need to be done in a balanced manner so the stress of taking on this responsibility didn't creep into my relationship the way it had in my previous marriage. For someone who had the history I did, this was a tall order.

In many ways I was a victim as a child. There was a lot of baggage associated with my parents' divorce, my domestic kidnapping, the dislocation of being smuggled out of my home country and having to adjust to a new family in a foreign land. My mother's alcoholism and early death, coupled with my own rebellion and foolish choices as a teenager and young man, had left me disadvantaged as I finally entered adulthood.

Much of what I had experienced since then, and the choices I had made, were an erratic and frustrating thrashing this way and that to free myself from psychological and emotional shackles holding me back. It had become clear to me that these shackles were largely of my own making, like an elephant that is trained as a baby with a stake that ties him to the ground. As an adult it would be a simple task to rip it out, but the elephant is bound, psychologically, to a belief that it can't be done.

Thirty years of active reflection had helped me cast off many of these psychological chains. I was at a point where I was largely freed up from restrictions that had been placed upon my spiritual well-being. But like many people are, I was still shackled in various ways by my own ego and desire, which made it difficult to serve God and my fellow human beings with a pure heart. Bob Dylan expresses this quite powerfully in his Grammy award–winning song "You Gotta Serve Somebody."

Unfortunately, John Lennon, like so many of us, seemed to miss the point of God, religion, and what Dylan was saying about submission. He called the song "embarrassing" and wrote "Serve Yourself" in response. [9] It was one of

9 "Gotta Serve Somebody," SongFacts, http://www.songfacts.com/detail.php?id=2935.

the last songs John recorded: "Serve Yourself" and "Dear John" are the last two songs released under his name.[10] His final messages were a rant against God and religion, and a letter to himself about not being so hard on himself since the race was over and he had won.

Dylan and Lennon are two of the greatest poets, musicians, and lyricists of the last one hundred years. They spoke to the hearts and souls of an entire generation and beyond. Dylan's take, versus Lennon's, is the one that rang true with me at a spiritual level. The Bible teaches freedom through submission. Accepting that you must serve others, rather than yourself, is relatively easy, but the devil is in the details. Finding the right balance between taking care of yourself while serving others is far more difficult.

Having finally won Angela's heart, our life together was precious. It was just like starting over. To avoid the mistakes that had led my first marriage to end in divorce, I needed figure out a way to achieve a relationship of mutual submission, the way God intended.

---

10 Robert Fontenot, "John Lennon's Last Song," ThoughtCo., updated August 19, 2017, https://www.thoughtco.com/john-lennons-last-song-2523035.

Come Together

Believe those who are seeking the truth. Doubt those who find it.
—André Gide

Material success enabled me to offer Angela a high degree of security and freedom. But even with a degree of material success, and despite—or perhaps because of—my strong religious beliefs, I had been unable to keep my ex-wife happy in our relationship. It would be easy to blame my childhood for this failure, but that would entail continuing to be a victim. Taking ownership of my mistakes was needed if I wanted my relationship with Angela to be different.

In order to understand where I had gone wrong in my former marriage I had to understand the flaws in my belief system. I knew the root of the problem was that I had swallowed a big lie about what the Bible teaches on the subject of male-female relationships. Reading the account of the creation of Adam and Eve with an open, inquisitive mind now, it is easy to see what the problem was.

WHEN I'M 64

The Bible opens with a beautiful creation story, in which God creates the earth as a verdant island in space. The first astronauts to view this sparkling blue gem were at a loss for words. And this whole planet was given to the first humans. Man and woman were both created in the image of God, placed in a pristine garden called Eden, with everything they needed at their fingertips.

They were as perfect for each other as everything else on the beautiful planet God gave them as their wedding gift.[1]

The human species is the pinnacle of creation. Our capacity, consciousness, free will, imagination, and creative power seem to have no limit. We were designed by God to be able to "subdue" the earth, to have "dominion" over everything in it. A greater and a lesser light were put in place to watch over us, like a gigantic mobile above the nursery created for our species. The lights in heaven were to govern us, as described by the words "to rule the day, and … the night" and "let them be for signs, and for seasons, and for days, and years."[2]

The symbolism is perfect, simple, and beautiful. The lights show us the way, in the daytime and even at night. Which brings us back to the article on the zodiac in the opening section. The author stated that "signs" referred to using stars for navigation, as in traversing the ocean. But this limitation is clearly incorrect, as the word for sign in Hebrew, *'owth*, means "a signal (literally or figuratively), as a flag, beacon, monument, omen, prodigy, evidence, etc.:— mark, miracle, (en-) sign, token". In other words, they serve a navigation function in the same manner across the ocean of time as well.[3]

And they also function as a clock to guide humankind through history. In matters big and small, immediate and long-term, physical and spiritual, we are to submit to the light, and not live in darkness. Just as wild beasts resist our efforts to tame them, our species struggles with submission to what God wants us to do. And yet, despite our resistance to it, the path forward is woven into the DNA of all creation.

Signs are mentioned first, illustrating how the calendar created by the motion of heavenly bodies is imbued with meaning. Since God created all this, which modern physics recognizes as space-time, it is self-evident that He exists outside it—and has full visibility into everything that ever has happened or ever will happen. And He has provided a map for those inside it, of history written in advance. His revealed Word works in conjunction with all creation—through the signs attached to the seasons, days, and years. God

1 Genesis 1:27 states, "So God created man in his own image, in the image of God created he him; male and female created he them." The first verse of the Shema illustrates the Jewish understanding of God: "Hear, O Israel: The LORD our God, the LORD is one" (Deuteronomy 6:4 NKJV). But that singular Being created two distinct members of the species, in His image. Genesis 1:28 makes it emphatic that they were sovereign over the entire physical creation on earth, just as God is sovereign in the highest. "And God blessed them, and God said unto them, Be fruitful, and multiply, and replenish the earth, and subdue it: and have dominion over the fish of the sea, and over the fowl of the air, and over every living thing that moveth upon the earth."
2 Genesis 1:14-18: "Then God said, 'Let there be lights in the firmament of the heavens to divide the day from the night; and let them be for signs and seasons, and for days and years; and let them be for lights in the firmament of the heavens to give light on the earth'; and it was so. Then God made two great lights: the greater light to rule the day, and the lesser light to rule the night. He made the stars also. God set them in the firmament of the heavens to give light on the earth, and to rule over the day and over the night, and to divide the light from the darkness" (NKJV).
3 Strong's Hebrew Lexicon (KJV), s.v. "H226, 'owth," accessed May 14, 2018, https://www.blueletterbible.org/lang/lexicon/lexicon.cfm?Strongs=H226&t=KJV.

later gives examples of how this works. Taken as a whole, the signs highlight the prophetic power of creation, which functions as a gigantic, prophetic clock.

One of the first prophetic lessons for infant humankind was on the relationship of men and women. Both are created in God's image, and each has different aspects of God featured more prominently in their composition. The differences are big, and they go very deep. The most obvious are the different reproductive organs, including the ability of women to bear children and to provide milk.

But estrogen and testosterone don't just create significant differences in our bodies; they also affect our brains and the way we move, act, think, and feel. Some studies, for example, illustrate that testosterone in the womb severs connections between the hemispheres, giving rise to the humorous, in some situations, observation that men are brain damaged. Conversely, women have greater connectivity between the hemispheres. The pros and cons that go along with having connections across the hemispheres include a more direct correlation among emotions and memories, relationships, and identity. There is a great power in how male and female brains, our operating systems, are structured. And of course, these manifest powerful differences between us.

These differences, when working together as a harmonious whole, can make a male-female union in marriage unstoppable and unshakable. Unfortunately, this pinnacle of creation decided to take a path not recommended by the manufacturer. A failure to submit to the light—the revelation and the laws of God—is to live in darkness. A general refusal to submit to the guiding lights God gave us is evident in individuals, families, tribes, and nations. It is endemic and systemic throughout human society. And it all began with a failure in the intended relationship between men and women.

As we move on through the book of Genesis we learn that God offered Adam and Eve a choice between the Tree of Life and the Tree of the Knowledge of Good and Evil. Here the prophetic component is a simple statement on what would happen if they ate from the wrong tree. It carried with it a death sentence. Eve listens to the serpent and chooses to disobey God. She convinces Adam to join her in sin. God pronounces judgment on the three of them in Genesis 3:14-19, projecting forward in time, with numerous prophetic elements.[4]

---

4 "And the Lord God said unto the serpent, Because thou hast done this, thou art cursed above all cattle, and above every beast of the field; upon thy belly shalt thou go, and dust shalt thou eat all the days of thy life: And I will put enmity between thee and the woman, and between thy seed and her seed; it shall bruise thy head, and thou shalt bruise his heel. Unto the woman he said, I will greatly multiply thy sorrow and thy conception; in sorrow thou shalt bring forth children; and thy desire shall be to thy husband, and he shall rule over thee. And unto Adam he said, Because thou hast hearkened unto the voice of thy wife, and hast eaten of the tree, of which I commanded thee, saying, thou shalt not eat of it: cursed is the ground for thy sake; in sorrow shalt thou eat of it all the days of thy life; thorns also and thistles shall it bring forth to thee; and thou shalt eat the herb of the field; in the sweat of thy face shalt thou eat bread, till thou return unto the ground; for out of it wast thou taken: for dust thou art, and unto dust shalt thou return."

PLEASE PLEASE ME

Much Christian discussion of God's judgment focuses on the childbirth aspect—and the enmity with the serpent, due to theological constructs around Jesus. But I'd like to focus here on two words in the statement "thy desire shall be to thy husband, and he shall rule over thee." Here the word "rule" is used for the second time. We had been told that the lights were to rule humankind. Now the concept of rulership among or within humankind is introduced for the first time. This judgment is really a prophetic prediction. The role of the woman is suppressed, and men would tend to dominate in the relationship. Family relationships became dysfunctional.

History, Scripture, and personal experience bear this out. In my case, my parents divorced at a crucial time in my childhood, resulting in an international kidnapping and a court battle that went to the Supreme Court of Sweden. Much of my life was spent recovering and trying to find my path forward.

My first marriage was burdened by the baggage of my childhood, but what destroyed it was the arrogance I brought to it, related to my false understanding of male-female relationships. This understanding was derived from the bizarre idea that the prophetic judgment resulting from turning away from God was a good thing. The husband was, in this scenario, in a role of divine authority. God was exercising His dominion through the man, in the marriage relationship. This idea had its roots in a wrong interpretation of the Genesis story.

The two uses of the word "rule" in such close proximity in this monumental origins section of the Word of God, where almost every word has powerful prophetic implications, creates an undeniable connection between Genesis 1:28 and 3:16. The former verse shows that Eve had equal stature with Adam over the earth and all that is in it, in submission to the light. As a result of her and Adam's actions, a change is introduced, leading us to the word "desire" (*tĕshuwqah*), which also reveals a prophetic unfolding of space-time. The definition of desire is a "longing, craving," and in the Bible it applies to a "man for woman," a "woman for man," and "of beast to devour."[5]

The original pristine state is harmony between men and women and with all creation. The next verses set vegetarian limits on what could be eaten, both by human and beast.[6] The dominion God intended for humans didn't include

5 Strong's *Hebrew Lexicon (KJV)*, s.v. "H8669, *tĕshuwqah*," accessed May 10, 2018, https://www.blueletterbible.org/lang/lexicon/lexicon.cfm?Strongs=H8669&t=KJV.

6 Genesis 1:29-30: "And God said, Behold, I have given you every herb bearing seed, which is upon the face of all the earth, and every tree, in the which is the fruit of a tree yielding seed; to you it shall be for meat. And to every beast of the earth, and to every fowl of the air, and to every thing that creepeth upon the earth, wherein there is life, I have given every green herb for meat: and it was so."

license to kill and eat their fellow creatures. Desire changes everything.

One of the most fascinating aspects to me is that *apostrephó* is the Greek word for desire, and it means "to turn away, turn back".[7] This key word is interwoven throughout the narrative—first Eve desires the forbidden fruit and turns her desire toward the man. In turning away from the light, she loses her sovereignty, and Adam begins to rule over her. Both Eve and Adam, in turning away from God, would have a long, long, long row to hoe, in a variety of ways.

Men and women can be caught up in fairy tale-style fantasies in which this judgment state of dysfunction seems like good thing. The codependency of damsels in distress and their rescuing white knights is but a form of mutual enslavement, one that all too often finds them not living happily ever after. Historically, grim, workaholic, underachieving men feel responsible for women whom the men simultaneously lean upon as a glorified serf. Add religious views like the ones about male leadership and female subservience I had only recently abandoned, and the enslavement is compounded.

God continues the pattern of delivering prophetic warnings by telling Cain that sin desires him. For Cain to regain his own sovereignty, God tells him he needs to rule over sin. That doesn't happen, and in his jealousy, Cain kills his righteous brother. Thus, God's prophetic statement regarding a magnification of Eve's sorrow in conception and childbirth quickly extends beyond the pain involved in delivering a baby. This sorrow surely grew infinitely worse as her firstborn son murdered her younger son, and then became an outcast. Then her daughters and their daughters were brought under brutal domination to the surviving sons and their sons (the ones who kill off the righteous ones) throughout history.

Our turning away from the light quickly turns into a downward spiral, away from God and the earthly sovereignty He granted each individual, toward an increasingly dark slavery to desire, sin, and each other. Once outside the garden, man officially becomes a carnivore, further cementing an aggregate result of the dynamic. The result of desire is that man and beast figuratively and literally begin to devour one another. And those who are capable of subduing and enslaving others proceed to do so in increasingly sophisticated ways, throughout recorded history.

---

7 *Strong's Greek Lexicon (KJV)*, s.v. "G654, apostrephō," accessed May 14, 2018, https://www.blueletterbible.org/lang/lexicon/lexicon.cfm?Strongs=G654&t=KJV- The Greek translation is called the Septuagint—Latin for "Seventy"— and the tradition around this translation, the first known Greek translation, is that 70 Jewish scholars translated it in the 3rd and 2nd centuries BC.

WHILE MY GUITAR GENTLY WEEPS

The mighty signature of God on the Genesis account is in evidence in the weave of forward-looking fulfillment of these trajectories, illustrated by examples of subjugation. Further examples build on this theme in an amazingly rich and complex way. The species God created in His image will soon challenge even the authority assigned to the heavenly lights, which have God-given dominion over us. This is in evidence in the attempt to build a tower to heaven at Bab El. We can easily infer from the biblical narrative that Nimrod subjugated others to the task of building the tower.[8] His city and his efforts are a prophetic marker for what later becomes Babylon, which is where Israel would later end up in captivity, and in the end times, Babylon the Great.

Moving forward in the story, notice how Joseph's brethren say to him, "Shalt thou indeed reign over us? or shalt thou indeed have dominion over us? And they hated him yet the more for his dreams, and for his words."[9] After acting on that hate, they sold Joseph into slavery. God, however, sets Joseph up in Egypt, and they are, indeed, brought under his sovereignty. The brothers resisted Joseph's destiny, and their hatred led them to the sin that resulted in Joseph having dominion over them. Ultimately all of Israel is brought under a most brutal oppression, by a Pharaoh whose heart God hardens. God then sends Moses to rescue Israel and end the dominion of Pharaoh while baptizing all of Israel in the Red Sea. The baptism of Israel is a prophetic example of the freedom that would come with the Savior, Christ, whose sacrifice would turn humanity back toward the light.

These are but a series of random snapshots that show the plant sprouting from the prophetic seed of Genesis. As it germinates and sprouts, it reveals the shoots, stalks, leaves, and buds that will yield the fruit of the arrival of the second Adam—the Messiah, Jesus—who begins the reversal of the trend of humanity's desire leading to constant subjugation.

Being hyperaware of having failed my ex-wife in many ways, I was very focused on learning how to treat Angela as my equal, with equal responsibility before God. What this looks like in action might seem obvious to others but for me it took self-analysis and alterations to my core identity and belief systems as I worked to wrap my head around new ideas.

Angela had recently completed a master's degree in physical therapy and was carrying a bit of a debt load from her studies. And we lived in an expensive area. Thankfully, I had been steadily moving up the corporate ladder and enjoyed

---

8 Genesis 10:8-10 discusses the beginning of the kingdom of "Nimrod the mighty hunter before the Lord." And the first of many famous cities he built was Babel.
9 Genesis 37:8.

the material benefits of that success, which gave me confidence in being able to fulfill some of the expectations my wife would have. But we were most focused on spiritual concerns. For me, what I continued to learn through my intentional involvement in big business augmented what I was learning through the lens of my God-and Bible-based value system.

For a while it had felt as though God was helping me fight and win various battles in my career. My image of myself was shaped by Joseph and Daniel—put in positions of power in Egypt and Babylon, respectively, to play roles on the divine stage. My career was a portal to learn what did and did not work in administering business affairs at a high level and to gain insight into the global system of materialism called Babylon the Great in the book of Revelation. Daniel's Babylon was a prophetic forerunner of this end-time Babylon, which had taken the people of God hostage, enslaving them along with the rest of humanity.

Biblical role models like Joseph and Daniel served the pinnacle of power in their day, economic and otherwise, while standing out as exceptional examples of service to God. In fact, they used their positions of proximity to the top of the material mountain to further the work of God in their respective times and places. So I worked very hard to advance in my understanding of and contribution to Countrywide's success. And at the same time, I continued my lifetime practice of reviewing my actions on a daily basis to ensure they conformed to my spiritual understanding. In this way I hoped to maintain my equilibrium and avoid being enslaved by the system I was working in. What I was learning, looking over Angela's shoulder as she investigated the Bahá'í faith, was very valuable in this balancing act.

One of the verses from the Bahá'í writings that made a big impression on me was from a little book called *The Hidden Words of Bahá'u'lláh*, translated from Arabic. The hidden words were proverb-length snippets that, according to Bahá'u'lláh's mini-preface, summarize the spiritual truth revealed throughout history. Bahá'u'lláh declares that "the inner essence thereof" was "clothed in the garment of brevity, as a token of grace unto the righteous."

I took to carrying this tiny volume around with me because the mini-messages did seem to condense the essence of truth in an astounding way. I committed the first Hidden Word to memory, a task made simple not only because of my attraction to the idea it expressed, and its relevance to my journey but also because of a song.

I had run into Devon Gundry, the performer of the prayer that had so moved me at a Bahá'í concert, and I had purchased his CD. Devon had married the first Hidden Word to a catchy tune. The text is "O Son of Spirit! My first counsel is this: Possess a pure, kindly and radiant heart, that thine may be sovereignty ancient, imperishable and everlasting." This did encapsulate much of what I had learned about the book of Genesis, Adam and Eve, sovereignty, submission to the light, and more.

As I approached my second wedding, the pain and fear generated from my painful divorce were eased by this surprising allusion to what my research had revealed about the God-given nature of male-female relationships. The symbols we had chosen for our wedding—the moon and the tide—illustrated my change of heart. It was even more joyous to know we were both submitting ourselves to the light, symbolized by the "greater and lesser light"—the sun and moon. These threads were about to come together in a way that would alter my perception of God, men, women, civilization, and the prophetic framework I was beginning to understand more fully.

ACROSS THE UNIVERSE

The Bahá'í Faith also taught the unity of religion and science, which reinforced my desire to study the connection between the two. Long gone was my fundamentalist aversion to what God could reveal to those engaged in scientific inquiry. So I pondered how God's love for His creation was at the heart of the process of evolution. Love is the primary energy behind the unfolding of His creation. At risk of oversimplifying love as a primary force, I defined it simply as attraction.

I couldn't explain exactly how it worked, but I began to meditate on how God's love, in the form of attraction, manifests itself in very subtle but very describable ways, even at the particle level. The laws that govern this process are built into the fractal patterns that permeate our universe, just as the principles revealed in Genesis are the fractal patterns that govern the unfolding of civilization.

Though there appear to be radically different rules or laws operating at that quantum level, even the amazingly weird actions at the tiniest subatomic level aggregate up to deliver this result at the particle, cellular, and human level. It's in our DNA and in our most sophisticated, educated, "adult" behavior.

Let me caveat that my thinking on this began a number of years prior to the release of the movie *The Secret*, which popularized the "law of attraction," among other things.[10] I am most certainly not promoting the movie, or agreeing

---

10 "The Secret is a 2006 film consisting of a series of interviews designed to demonstrate the New Thought claim that everything one wants or needs can be satisfied by believing in an outcome, repeatedly thinking about it, and maintaining positive emotional states to 'attract' the desired outcome." Wikipedia, s.v. "The Secret (2006 film)," last modified April 19, 2018, https://en.wikipedia.org/wiki/The_Secret_(2006_film).

with it, as it addresses a similar theme but with little, if any, reference to God and an inordinate emphasis on material success. But readers who have seen the movie may appreciate my attraction to the idea that Love operates as a fundamental force of attraction throughout the very fabric of the universe.

This love force originates from God and manifests itself, in various unfolding ways, in the attractive forces driving the evolution of the universe, which might be called the pre-physical qualities of matter. These forces, based on spiritual laws originating in God, coalesce into the bodies we know through both quantum and classical physics. The attraction of particles to each other and the formation of relationships between them resulted, after billions of years and the guiding force of God's love, in the arrival of life and reproduction. From that moment on, the eros type of love becomes an almost violently motivating attractive force in nature, driving the evolutionary process forward. It created living entities which, although unbelievably primitive at the beginning, were the result of billions of years of the aggregate results of God's creative plan in action. And the aggregate results of the evolutionary force of life, reproducing and advancing itself, continued accelerating the pace of that creative plan.

For me personally, I had become intensely attracted to Angela at a time when she was exploring Yoga, in her own quest for greater openness to a new spiritual path. Through Yoga she had been introduced to the Bahá'í Faith and had become attracted to it. When I first met Angela, my attraction to her was behind my eagerness to join her in attending a meeting about the Bahá'í faith.

The openness behind my thinly disguised reason for attending this meeting was challenged by my perception of the event as a thinly disguised attempt at indoctrination. The book Angela had been studying with the Bahá'í women's group hosting this meeting was already a tip-off. It was called *The Book of Certitude*—certitude being a sneaky substitute for the word "faith." In the meeting I attended, they used the archaic word "circumambulation." I decided to seek an explanation on why words that seemed to obscure the meaning were used in a meeting clearly designed to interest outsiders in an already obscure religion.

THE WORD

My critical approach to these words probably didn't endear me to those hosting the event, but my hunch was confirmed. Certitude meant faith, and circumambulation described a practice of walking around something for religious purposes. As I reflected on this, my irritation at the clunky words gave way to fascination with the connections they brought to mind. The Israelites had walked around the walls of Jericho which brought the walls down, and then there was Stonehenge and my experience in a small village in the state of Tamil Nadu, India, called Tiruvannemalai.

In *The Hardness of the Heart* I told how an engine failure in our car had stranded my Indian friend Michael and I in a remote area of India. We had ended up sleeping on the dirty cement of an outdoor garage in this regional village when we were startled awake by the noise created by a large procession. We were enclosed within the outer edge of a circle of worship in which believers honored their god by circumambulating the mountain at whose base we happened to be trying to sleep. This was a memorable experience, and now it was emerging as a turning point in my understanding.

Was there something important in a practice that to Western-educated minds could so easily be dismissed as walking in circles?

The architecture of the universe, from its smallest to its largest systems, is based on orbits being established and aggregated by the forces that create them and which they create. And while I had lived my life knowing that God used the laws He built into the natural order to bring us into harmony with Him, I had never previously considered that He had instituted a religious practice to integrate the physical and spiritual.

Two of the questions I found most interesting in my sporadic research into scientific topics was how consciousness arises and its relationship to free will. My particular focus was the degree to which individuals are sovereign and can shape our reality, based on being created in God's image. These thoughts had been sparked by my research into quantum mechanics. It had always seemed to me that the way in which quantum particles ignored the laws of classical physics was similar to free will. As this manuscript goes to my editor, scientists are beginning to explore these connections.[11]

Like humans, quantum particles are free to behave across an entire spectrum of options. With these particles, until they are observed, any and all of their options are possible. Only after their choice has been observed does it become a fixed reality—this is known as the wave function collapse.

I had come to view humans, in terms of God's plan, like these particles. As God is establishing His Kingdom, it awaits the conversion and subsequent

11 George Musser, "The Quantum Physics of Free Will," *Scientific American*, February 6, 2012, https://www.scientificamerican.com/article/quantum-physics-free-will/.

obedience of humans who, at this stage, are free to disobey the laws of God and behave irrationally. The quantum state of particles illustrates, in nature, how God has enabled a system in which free will exists at a particle (individual) level, but as matter aggregates up, the wave function collapses and matter conforms to the laws of classical physics.

So it is with humans.

Eve, then Adam, had a binary option—to eat or not eat of the fruit God had forbidden. And when they chose to eat, it was a catalyst that set the course of the evolution of humankind. Adam's sons Cain and Abel also made choices, and Cain chose to introduce murder. These events illustrate how free will, over time, as civilization advances, aggregates the decisions that are made and thereby forces development in a negative direction.

The Bahá'ís I was meeting with believed, as the Bible outlines, that along the way, God has sent His messengers and prophets to reveal to us that which will lead to alignment with His plan. These messengers and prophets direct our attention to the light, but because we have free will, we shy away from the stark reality of what it reveals—or even willfully turn away from it. Even when we try to obey, we're imperfect, and the aggregations of our intent to obey result in large-scale religions that are utterly corrupt and ultimately have to be destroyed. The Bible reveals this about ancient Israel, and history shows that the same is true of Christianity.

ALL THINGS MUST PASS

Christian history, at least in the West, is dominated by the Catholic Church. Catholic means universal, and the Church's traditional theology lays claim to being the only door to salvation. It is not unique in its claims, as many churches, like the WCG, of which I had been a part, suffer under the delusional arrogance of believing they are the one and only true church. But the Catholic Church took this affront to God and humankind to an extraordinary level by declaring itself to be the Kingdom of God on earth. It set itself up as infallible, granting itself the right to interpret and even overturn the previously revealed Word of God.

Small wonder that the Catholic Church vilified Galileo and Copernicus for daring to confront the power of the church over the idea that the earth circulates around our sun, the source of light, heat, and life itself. The aggregation of *tĕshuwqah*, turning away from the light, led to the "universal church" presiding over a descent into what fittingly became known as the Dark Ages.

Today, we are seeing this pattern writ very large across the global stage, with Islam. The religion of Islam appears not only to have fallen from its zenith, in which it arguably played a role in helping Western civilization recover from the Dark Ages, but today large areas of the Islamic world seem to have reached a crescendo of blindness and corruption. Major Islamic movements are at war with both Judeo-Christian civilization and scientific materialism. Modern science should be leading us into the light, but too often, in its rejection of God and moral absolutes, it is the latest outgrowth of humanity's attempt to resist submitting to the dominion of the greater and lesser light, thereby becoming enslaved by the pursuit of our own desires apart from the light.

Science has flourished as a result of rejecting these corrupt forms of religion. Science provides a human-devised method of determining the most rational way to behave. This is significantly not revealed directly, or imposed by God, but is rather an expression of the free will choice of human beings. Since God is the Creator of the universe, it will ultimately lead people, in great numbers, to Him, because all of creation is in fact just another revelation of God.

The observations of peer-reviewed scientists lead to agreement on modes of behavior, and the systems, rules, relationships, and structures are put in place that move a majority of people toward rational behavior. Nonetheless, the route that human reasoning takes is often fraught with error and becomes circuitous. For example, before science leads us to God, it may for a while lead us further away. It is the yin to religion's yang. And religion starts with God and then veers away.

Free will, exercised apart from or in opposition to revealed knowledge, often brings us to a "rock bottom." We observe the net effect of our decisions and conclude that we must change direction. Science can assist in informing and educating the choices to which we apply our free will. But science, unfortunately, generally rejects revelation entirely. Anyone who disallows the revelation of God's Word will be unable to use it as a feedback loop to calibrate what is learned from studying the creation.

And vice versa. Being open to revelation, science, and logic, I was benefitting from a virtuous feedback loop among these elements. Circumambulation is not only a metaphor for taking such feedback loops into account; it creates a feedback loop between the physical and the spiritual plane.

The practice of circumambulation, that strange word that irritated me in this first meeting with the Bahá'ís, was a very literal, physical act in which we bring ourselves into alignment with the laws of nature, in a religious context.

We behave like classical particles rather than free radicals. Rather than leaving our options open, when we determine to circumambulate, to walk with intent around a religious center, we objectively make visible a choice to obey a divine pattern that is revealed both in the abstract of divine guidance and in the structure of the physical, from particles and molecules on up to solar systems and galaxies. And this predictable behavior is at the heart of electromagnetics and gravity.

Interestingly, it all starts with the determination of whether an electron has a positive or a negative spin. This has an interesting correlation to modern human language, which is an expression of our evolving consciousness. My point is simply that circumambulation is how humankind brings itself into direct spiritual alignment with the patterns of orbits around orbits, indicated by the Earth's relationship to the Sun and the Moon, in conformity with the stars.

Of course, not all people are interested in aligning themselves with divine patterns. Many today deny the divine altogether. My evolving theory was that divine patterns established by the celestial clock God described in the opening chapter of Genesis as driven by the greater and lesser lights, along with the stars, would become manifest to science. In other words, science will one day assist in making the divine undeniable.

There is a misconception about Einstein's general theory of relativity. It is true that Einstein's special theory of relativity proved Newton's conception of absolute space and absolute time to be false. But Einstein himself actually wanted to distance his theory of general relativity from the popular implications of its name.[12] One of the achievements of Einstein was proving that the speed of light is a constant—it moves 671 million miles per hour, regardless of whether the observer is moving in any direction or speed. I often wonder why, given this fact, there is not more attention paid to the monumental statement in Genesis 1:3, "Let there be light."

In Einstein's model, space-time as a whole is, in fact, absolute—not relative, not subject to different perspectives and interpretations. While a person's negative or positive spin of a given event might encourage them to deny a specific prophetic fulfillment, the Bible makes a similar point about prophecy in this context: it is not subject to private interpretation.[13] To me, this highlights the importance of prophecy in determining a proper orientation in time and space. It is a constant that is more powerful and valuable than theological

12 "Consequently, Felix Klein (1910) called it the 'invariant theory of the Lorentz group' instead of relativity theory, and Einstein (who reportedly used expressions like 'absolute theory') sympathized with this expression as well." Wikipedia, s.v. "Criticism of the Theory of Relativity," last modified November 24, 1017, https://en.wikipedia.org/wiki/Criticism_of_the_theory_of_relativity#cite_ref-84.

13 2 Peter 1:20: "Knowing this first, that no prophecy of the scripture is of any private interpretation."

interpretations, creeds, beliefs, and those things religion has tended to elevate above common sense, human experience, and logic.

Even though I was enjoying having new inputs to my search for coherence, my fundamental concerns with participating in discussion with this unusual group were not so easily addressed. For starters, to state the obvious, the Bahá'í Faith was a religious belief system that was not Christianity. While this profoundly tested my newfound spiritual openness, my desire to orbit Angela's world forced me to at least pretend to be open. Also, despite my concerns, I knew it was right to mirror the friendly, open discussion I was experiencing, which enabled me to absorb a number of positive ideas and concepts provided by the Bahá'ís.

One of these positive ideas was the refreshing way in which they approached faith, which they called certitude, the word I had sarcastically dismissed. I was surprised to learn that the Bahá'í Faith not only asserts an essential unity of science and religion, but also insists on the independent investigation of truth. I was intrigued by these dual principles and impressed with their succinct and elegant summaries of conclusions it had taken me painful decades to arrive at on my own.

The discussion, sponsored by the Bahá'í women's group, was also not what I had expected. My negative spin, going into it, was that a feminist approach was likely to be present. This did not materialize, nor did I sense any tension or negative undercurrent between testosterone-and estrogen-fueled perspectives. A Bahá'í emphasis on the principle of the equality of men and women certainly contributed to this, and this was beautifully illustrated by the metaphor of men and women being the "two wings of one bird." The Bahá'ís seemed to bring their principles to life in a way that warmed the heart.

As the attendees began to pose questions, the organizers introduced something they called "Bahá'í consultation." This method relies on the concept of detachment, which was another concept foreign to my experience. I had formed intense attachment to the spiritual values and ideas I had embraced. Detachment, in Bahá'í consultation, means participant contributions are accepted, not argued with. They are "laid on the table" and the contributor is expected to detach from his or her idea. All group members then discuss all ideas in an effort to arrive at a more complete truth. Here those of different persuasions might come together, so that proponents of three divergent ideas might, instead of arguing, reach a conclusion that one and one and one is three.

I had been looking for people who were open to religious discussion apart from preconceived ideas. But was their detachment real, or was this some kind of sophisticated handling—a method of indoctrination to the cult? Since Bahá'ís believed in the essential unity of science and religion, it seemed appropriate to put them to the test.

I'll Follow the Sun

We used to think agriculture gave rise to cities and later to writing, art, and religion. Now the world's oldest temple suggests the urge to
worship sparked civilization.
—CHARLES C. MANN

It was only a matter of minutes before I got the chance to test the Bahá'ís on an important topic.

A young Baptist woman attending the discussion group asked about making a donation. Most Baptists teach tithing—giving a tenth of one's increase to God. The Worldwide Church of God taught that 10 percent of our gross income was holy, and to withhold it was stealing from God. Since the WCG was God's church, the logic went, it was authorized to collect tithes and offerings.

Seeing people suffer under this administration had led me to examine the relevant verses more critically. When it became clear the church's practice did not even come close to conforming to what the Bible said, I resigned from the full-time ministry to separate my paycheck from my faith. I could no longer live with myself while living off the member's tithes.

WHAT GOES ON

The Baptist woman was told that donations to the Bahá'í Faith are not accepted from non-Bahá'ís. This caught my interest, so I asked how the group was funded and how the money was allocated and spent. In the process I learned that the Bahá'ís have no clergy, and aside from a relatively tiny percentage of people in administrative roles, nobody depended on the Bahá'í Faith for their livelihood.

This was a pleasant surprise, but I dug further. There were global, national and local organizations, each funded by voluntary donations at these various levels. "Is there no such thing as a required donation?" I asked. The answer was yes: there was a Bahá'í law which stipulated that a percentage of one's aggregate wealth was to be contributed as it was earned, or at a set time of the member's choosing.

This was in alignment with tithing as outlined in the covenant Moses brought. In that model, a land grant from God supported the requirement to tithe on the increase from the land. In the modern world, this is the equivalent of a capital gains tax versus an income tax—very much in line with what the Bahá'ís taught. They were only expected to contribute on the increase they enjoyed after all living expenses were deducted. While Bahá'ís were clearly in line with biblical principle on this, I wasn't done testing them.

"What if," I asked one of the main organizers, "I mailed a check to Bahá'í headquarters?"

"It would be returned with an explanation," she replied.

"Really," I blurted out somewhat incredulously. "They literally send it back."

"Yes" was the confident reply. "It happens all the time."

There was nowhere else to go with my line of questioning, so I let it go at that point, without making up my mind on whether this was a tactic, naiveté, or commitment to a higher principle.

There were a few other exchanges at the meeting, on topics that challenged my understanding a bit, and which I can't now specifically recall, but the idea that all religions come from God was a primary sticking point. Bahá'ís seemed to interpret the Bible in symbolic terms which allowed them to embrace wishful platitudes. What impressed me, though, was the sincerity of their belief. Whether it appeared wise or naive from my perspective, there did not appear to be any internal logical conflict in the key beliefs they professed. And while I disagreed with the idea that all religions came from God, Bahá'í beliefs about the unity of religion and science and the independent investigation of truth were important positives.

These two pillars were supported by the platforms of detachment and Bahá'í consultation. This all made perfect sense and was wonderful to experience in action. All my questions were treated with the utmost respect, and there was no condescending dismissal of what I presented, even if it conflicted with their ideas. In fact, I had the distinct feeling that one or two of the participants had been at least as open, if not more so, to my ideas than I had been to theirs. This was both refreshing and encouraging. I saw no reason not to continue to accompany

Angela, as she continued to strengthen her ties to these people and their beliefs. And there was a particular element of Bahá'í history that had really piqued my interest.

SOMETHING

The Bahá'ís told me that they viewed the Báb, the Gate of God referenced earlier, as a John-the-Baptist-like figure whose purpose it was to announce the arrival of Bahá'u'lláh. If there was any validity to the claims they were making, the Báb was the Elijah to come.[1]

The WCG had implied, if not outright claimed, that Herbert W. Armstrong had been the Elijah to come. *The People of the Sign* asks the question whether he fulfilled the pivotal prophecy about this Elijah with which the Old Testament ends. The book ultimately rejects it on the basis of Armstrong's failure to turn his own heart to his children, and theirs to him; this pattern of familial failure played out amongst a large cross section of his followers, including my own father.[2] I had not thought much about the Elijah to come since, but now I did.

As I've already explained, Báb means "gate," and El, in Hebrew, means "God"—as in El Shaddai ("God the Almighty") or Bethel ("house of God"). Since Babel is understood to mean "confusion", I had never focused on the El part of the name, but at the first opportunity I carefully read the familiar story in Genesis 11. It's worth reviewing here:

> And the whole earth was of one language, and of one speech. And it came to pass, as they journeyed from the east, that they found a plain in the land of Shinar; and they dwelt there. And they said one to another, Go to, let us make brick, and burn them thoroughly. And they had brick for stone, and slime had they for morter. And they said, Go to, let us build us a city and a tower, whose top may reach unto heaven; and let us make us a name, lest we be scattered abroad upon the face of the whole earth. And the LORD came down to see the city and the tower, which the children of men builded. And the LORD said, Behold, the people is one, and they have all one language; and this they begin to do: and now nothing will be restrained from them, which they have imagined to do. Go to, let us go down, and there confound their language, that they may not understand one another's speech. So the LORD scattered them abroad from thence upon the face of all the earth: and

---

1 Malachi 4:5: "Behold, I will send you Elijah the prophet before the coming of the great and dreadful day of the Lord."
2 Malachi 4:6: "And he will turn the hearts of the fathers to the children, and the hearts of the children to their fathers, lest I come and strike the earth with a curse" (NKJV).

they left off to build the city. Therefore is the name of it called Babel; because the LORD did there confound the language of all the earth: and from thence did the LORD scatter them abroad upon the face of all the earth.[3]

From my new perspective, I realized I had missed important details in this familiar story. The phrase "Tower of Babel" doesn't appear in the Bible because the story is actually about Nimrod's city and the intent of the people to establish a name for themselves. This city was the focus, as in "the city and the tower." Nimrod, in this context, was presumably striving to establish himself or his city as the Gate of God.[4] This is the origin of the term we know as Babylon.

The tradition around Nimrod supports this: his efforts were to establish greatness apart from God —a turning away from God. The tower, according to some of these traditions, was to evoke this greatness, to give the people gathering at Babylon a material symbol of his might and power to be impressed with, humbled by, and eventually enslaved by.

This is what God put a stop to, giving the city a name that was a divine pun. He substituted a similar-sounding word to enshrine the confusion of the language which stopped the endeavor. Instead of establishing a city called, in Akkadian, the "Gate of God," it is now known by the Hebrew Babel, from *Balal*, meaning "to mix, mingle, confuse, confound."[5]

The significance of the Báb's name, the Gate of God, was in being "the Primal Point" around which "the realities of the Prophets and Messengers revolve."[6] Bahá'ís believed that the Gate of God was bringing humanity back together, and that a global language would be established that would be instrumental in uniting humankind. There seemed to be more behind this Bab El / Babel irony than was evident on the surface.

His role, it appeared, was to somehow accomplish that which humankind had failed to do at the Tower of Babel. That Bahá'ís seemed unaware of any connection between the Gate of God and Babel just fueled my fascination. I couldn't shake the feeling that this was really important, and until I understood it, I couldn't resolve my nagging feeling that the Bahá'í Faith was a step in the wrong direction.

In an odd way, this fascination positively impacted the wedding planning efforts. In reflecting on my own life's experiences, I had already begun to think of music as a universal language, able to transcend linguistic and cultural differences. This led me to take a deep personal interest in the music for the wedding.

3 Genesis 11:1-9.
4 The word Babylon is derived from Akkadian bab (gate) + ilu (god). John L. McKenzie, Dictionary of the Bible (New York: Touchstone, 1965), s.v. "Tower of Babel."
5 *The NAS Old Testament Hebrew Lexicon, s.v. "Balal,"* accessed May 10, 2018, https://www.biblestudytools.com/lexicons/hebrew/nas/balal.html.
6 Shoghi Effendi, *God Passes By* (Wilmette: Bahá'í Publishing Trust, 1971), 57.

My dad and stepmother, who were still deeply attached to the ideas of the WCG movement, had dogmatic religious views. Mike Rochelle, who had remained a close friend despite religious differences of opinion, was my best man. My other groomsman, Mark Schnee, a close friend since our days together in Germany and an accomplished musician, had strong religious views that were distinct from mine as well. On the other side of the aisle would be Angela's Catholic family and some of her new Bahá'í friends. Angela's maid of honor, Syrisa, still attended a WCG splinter group in which I had been a minister. Paith, the Yoga friend who had introduced her to the Bahá'í faith, was her other bridesmaid. All these participants, along with many of the guests, would also be concerned about the tone of the religious ceremony, which Angela and I had yet to figure out. A careful use of music might bridge some of these differences and make the day more enjoyable and acceptable for all parties.

I took advantage of another chance meeting with Devon to let him know how much I liked his CD and to ask him if he would do me a favor. I had made several attempts in the past to compose songs, working with other musicians. Would he be willing to help me put a poem to music for my wedding? While my interest in him was in his music, he had an interest in my experience with business. Devon was working with a couple of friends on a new Internet concept, in the wake of the success of Myspace and its new competitor, a then little-known site called Facebook.

Devon and I got together to discuss, and in the process he agreed to help me compose a song based on the Moon/Tide poem. The initial results were very promising, and I hatched a plan to use it as a surprise serenade to Angela at our wedding dinner.

As excitement was building, week by week and month by month, during this slowly unfolding year of expectation, my career was slowly unraveling. Countrywide's mission to enable the average American to realize the American Dream, which had once appealed to me, now seemed like a sick joke. I described earlier how Countrywide's brilliant business strategy was both cynical and sinister.

I SHOULD HAVE KNOWN BETTER

There was nothing unethical about the strategy, per se, as it was perfectly in line with the intended role of a corporation. Once brought to life by its creators, it is given agency and power to grow very large and make obscene amounts of money. Its creators and owners reap the benefits and remain legally immune from any harm it creates. It's a nice update on the classic Frankenstein story. And the economic output of several of these corporations has grown larger than the entire output of most countries. Like sharks they must keep swimming to stay alive, and like the dinosaurs of old they have grown to enormous proportions.

This system of profit-driven materialism is ultimately posing a threat to civilization and destroying the planet in the process. Its defenders praise this system for its ability to create the jobs, wealth, goods, and services that we all crave. But this system exists in a symbiotic relationship with humankind, in our role as caretakers of the planet; we are in a codependent, materialistic death embrace.

The linguistic and contextual connection between Nimrod's Bab El and the "mighty city" Babylon is important. The biblical prophet Daniel was prominent in the court of Nebuchadnezzar, king of Babylon. I began to draw inspiration from what he accomplished while in that role. It gave a spiritual significance to what I was learning in my own little corner of Babylon the Great.

Throughout the ages many have speculated on exactly what is intended by the many references to Babylon the Great in the book of Revelation. This end-time Babylon trades in all manner of luxuries and delicacies. It eventually becomes so powerful and far reaching that it is described as trading in "bodies and souls of men." Babylon makes the "merchants of the earth" so rich that they will weep and mourn over her when "no man buyeth their merchandise any more."[7]

In today's world, to obtain the material benefits giant corporations deliver, people regularly sell out to these soulless entities. In MBA programs corporate culture is typically addressed in classes on organizational behavior. I took such a class in my MBA program and was assigned a paper comparing and contrasting two corporate cultures. Given what I was coming to understand about the company I worked for, I chose to compare Countrywide culture to the Mafia.

The Mafia requires what is known as a drone, an up-and-coming leader, to murder someone in order to secure some advantage or protection within "the family." Once the deed is accomplished, the murder weapon with the killer's fingerprints is kept in a safe—under the control of the head of the family. If you ever cross the boss, it won't be the boss who goes to jail. Countrywide seemed to me to deploy similar tactics. As 2006 was coming to a close, the stakes were getting higher and higher.

Bloggers, analysts, and reporters were leveling increasing accusations against Mozilo's preplanned massive weekly stock sales. Then the President of Countrywide, Mozilo's long-time friend, and heir apparent, was ousted, as

---

7 Revelation, chapter 18.

Countrywide's board (of which Mozilo was chairman) and management (of which Mozilo was CEO) announced a billion-dollar stock-buyback program. This was at the peak of the housing bubble, when the trading community knew that Countrywide stock was already at inflated prices, and more and more investors were piling on to short it.

But Mozilo still had more he wanted to sell, and he was in a position to dictate that, even if nobody else wanted to buy the stock, the company would help him out. In other words, the net effect of the buyback program was to keep the stock at its inflated historic highs. This enabled Angelo to sell his personal stock into the demand created by the company, which he controlled, even though the market was shorting the stock. This seemed to me to be a direct, concerted, and grossly unethical effort to siphon money out of the organization he had built.

The parallel between our global economy and Revelation had already been highlighted, in my view, by the collapse of the twin towers at the hand of radical Islam. The slow, sequential collapse of these two buildings seemed an unmistakable prophetic indicator that we were close to the time when the immortal line "Babylon the Great is fallen, is fallen" would be fulfilled. It was a judgment against American-style capitalism in the wake of ever-growing excesses and the way in which the scale of large corporations was increasingly complicating global geopolitics. My experience at Countrywide had become the most striking example yet.

The CEO had recently been invited to ring the opening bell on Wall Street, and there I was, in a strategic leadership role in one of the fastest-growing companies in the most prosperous nation the world had ever seen. I was helping develop plans to enable even greater success. I was giving it my all, and for a while it seemed that my contributions were making a difference.

Yet, in late 2006, my efforts to pursue a spiritual course from within a corrupt entity hit a brick wall as I came to see the company as essentially evil, causing a great degree of inner turmoil. As a result, I was now having increasing trouble charting my own course within the company. In January 2007, I found myself so at odds with management that my relationship with this economic powerhouse was abruptly severed. My success at Countrywide ended with me being escorted out of the building.

This was a devastating blow.

HELP!

For a while it had felt as though God was helping me fight and win various battles as I ascended the corporate ladder. I had moved up inside the global system of materialism called Babylon the Great, of which Joseph's Egypt and Daniel's Babylon were prophetic forerunners. Now I had been cast out.

My ejection from Countrywide was due, I felt, at some deep level, to my own failure to learn from past mistakes. The corporate world is highly competitive, with material rewards so great that the worst in us is often on vivid display. Employees fight and squabble to obtain the best position to obtain these rewards. In this environment my biggest challenge had been the arrogance inherent in believing that God would protect me, even as qualities like humility, politeness, and courtesy were often used in an insincere way by others, and thus undervalued, even by me.

My own inability to navigate and negotiate through the difficult culture had caused this failure. God had offered an apprenticeship with some similarity to Daniel's, but I hadn't made the cut. My feelings of guilt and shame at having failed, materially and spiritually, weighed even more heavily on me than the financial uncertainty the failure caused, just as I was committing myself to major expenses.

Had I known a global economic meltdown was just around the corner, I might have been even more concerned about our finances. On the other hand, perhaps I should have been easier on myself. Rather than failing, perhaps I was more like Daniel escaping the lion's den.

Countrywide was a major earthquake behind the financial tsunami that began to roll across the globe in 2008. I was ejected right before it hit. Shortly after I left, in quick succession, Countrywide virtually collapsed and was acquired at bargain-basement prices by Bank of America. Mozilo was labeled by *Time* magazine in January 2009, as the number-one cause of the economic meltdown. Then the series of articles by Matt Taibbi in *Rolling Stone* magazine skewered him and other key corporate villains, as well as various components of what I've been calling the system of systems.[8] Even if they weren't calling it Babylon the Great, an increasingly large segment of the population was realizing that our economic system had the entire planet in a stranglehold.

Annie Leonard, who became famous when her *Story of Stuff* video went viral on the Internet, wrote an article titled "The Human Cost of Stuff." It featured interviews with Haitians who ended up in garment factories when their

---

8 Matt Taibbi is but the most colorful of writers and filmmakers who exposed the robo-signing scandal and other banking and corporate criminal excesses committed by the firms that contributed to the great recession, in a variety of books, articles, and documentaries.

ability to support themselves on their farms was undermined by cheap rice from the US. They were convinced they were the victims of a conspiracy involving the World Bank and the US Agency for International Development to create third-world factories serving rich Americans. Annie writes, "My jaw dropped as the man from the USAID agency openly agreed with what at first had sounded like an exaggerated conspiracy theory."[9]

Does the naturally selfish behavior of individuals and groups qualify as a conspiracy? I believe in some sense it does. The Holy Spirit tries to urge us to behave unselfishly, but this is more difficult to do as a society than one can imagine. Western/capitalistic economic theory is based on self-interest. In our society, individuals dedicated to altruism are salmon swimming upstream. In 2007, for example, I read a quote attributed to Warren Buffet that said, "Trickle-down Economics works, but the rich have found a way to plug the leaks."

Corporate interests, in the US in particular, have got the electorate believing in a free market system that they, in fact, largely control. We tend to believe in this free market ideology because it somehow resonates with our desires, but we're not looking at it holistically or objectively. It is another way in which we turn away from the light. We deceive ourselves that this system of systems benefits us, as it panders to our material desires. As we worship it, we make micro and macro decisions that are opposed to our own best interest, further entrenching our enslavement to the rich and powerful forces that are aggregated up in the system known as Babylon.

Joseph and Daniel were important because they were involved in the inner workings of the governmental and economic power centers of their respective civilizations. Within those systems they were used to uphold and reflect a different set of standards from those in the world around them. I had viewed myself as following in their footsteps, a personal adaptation of the theological framework of the WCG movement that gave me comfort. Now I had to admit my beliefs had led me to a dead end in my marriage, my religious affiliation, and finally, my career.

All of this added up to a general uneasiness about my spiritual future. Even so, I still felt tantalizingly close to a "connect-the-dots" framework, as though an image was being revealed, just beyond my ability to perceive it. There had to be a lens somewhere that would provide coherence.

---

9 Annie Leonard, "The Human Cost of Stuff," YES!, Fall 2013.

WHEN I GET HOME

I was reminded of a short story I read years earlier, by science fiction writer Ray Bradbury.[10] Starship captain Hart arrives on a planet shortly after a nameless Savior had visited. Most of his crew becomes enamored with the new community of believers and decides to stay, happy to bask in the reflected glow of a community that had been touched by the Man. The Captain is not content with this, and much of the story finds him debating with fellow interstellar explorer Martin about the value of staying versus leaving.

Hart reboards the ship with a few loyal crew members to chase the Man across the galaxy, wanting to come face-to-face with him. The narrator reveals that Hart is destined to get closer in his search, missing him by weeks, then days, then hours, then seconds, but never quite catching him. I could identify both with Captain Hart's desperate but ultimately fruitless search and with Martin, who found what he was looking for.

For me, the WCG had once provided the community Martin had experienced. The WCG had been global, tight knit, and loving. The Sign of the Sabbath had been held near and dear, and under that banner I had traveled across the planet, from above the Arctic Circle in Alaska and Sweden to the southern reaches of apartheid South Africa. I had ascended from the lowest point on earth, the Dead Sea, to mountain peaks on several continents. I had circled the earth from the land of the rising sun in the East, to India, to the westernmost islands of the Pacific. No matter where I was, WCG members understood and obeyed the Sign, proving to us that we were God's special, chosen people. We had basked in the glow of that knowledge and in our fellowship with one another on the Sabbath, under the reflected light of the annual Holy Days of the Hebrew calendar, determined by the moon.

After learning that the WCG was not what it had claimed to be, it still had taken years for me to recognize that Jesus had brought a new Sign for His followers. The Sabbath yielded its role as the identifying Sign, in favor of different Signs for who He was and how to recognize His followers. My world travels were now largely over. Like Martin, I had realized that the answer for me was to stay in one place. The idea that the law of God was absolute and unchanging across the millennia had been comforting, and the complications and contradictions inherent in realizing that the application of law changes over time left me unsettled. And in gaining insight into the flaws in the claims made by the WCG and its splinter groups, I had no choice but to behave more like Hart—to leave this community in search of one that followed God's direction.

---

10 "Ray Bradbury, *"The Man,"* in The Illustrated Man (New York: Simon & Schuster, 1981), 62-77.

I was on a search for better answers. And like Hart, I felt like I was getting closer. Reflecting on how Israel missed the arrival of the Messiah was how I took one step forward.

Christ was the Promised Rest that they had observed through the symbolic setting aside of one day a week for God. The Sabbath was the Sign, the symbol, not the reality. The WCG movement had this backward. The permanent relationship with Christ was the reality, and the temporary law of the Sabbath under Moses's covenant was the particular stamp of identity that marked them as the people to whom Christ would come. Unfortunately for Israel, they rejected the reality of their covenant in favor of their flawed understanding of its Sign. I was now coming to understand that I had been doing this same thing.

WORKING CLASS HERO

But where should I go next? I had no interest in joining a group with the same problems I'd been fighting. All religious groups seemed to have fallen victim to hierarchical structures of control, manipulation, domination, the hypocrisy of teachings designed to pass judgment on others, egos, and wrong-headed politics, not to mention major doctrinal error and outright backward interpretation of Scripture.

The Bahá'ís were wonderful people, and it was comfortable to be around them, especially since their religion didn't seem to have most of these problems. But the idea that Christ had returned in secret, in Iran, was so laughable that I wasn't willing to seriously consider it. I very much enjoyed spending time with them, and it was opening up new perspectives, but I was itching to get serious about finding the truth.

Somewhere God had to be preparing for Christ's return, in some transcendent way, with people whose hearts were pure. This would be the spiritual edge of where He was moving His creation forward. But where? And how could a truly spiritual group even exist, in a material world gone so far astray?

And speaking of the material world, while I was trying to figure this out, my immediate challenge was finding a new job. I was now two months from a wedding, the costs for which had ballooned to enormous proportions. It would be followed by a honeymoon, which would take me and my bride to the islands of Fiji and on to New Zealand. All this extravagance had been set in motion while I was gainfully employed, a condition which had suddenly changed for the worse.

The good news is that, along with the rest of the country, I had bene-fitted from the hyperinflation of the real estate bubble. I had tapped into easy financing to acquire property in the right place at the right time. The stock market had been keeping pace, and I had made smart decisions there as well. My personal net worth had recovered from my divorce thirty months earlier and was trending north of a half-million dollars. The job market was also still hot, so I wasn't worried. In fact, once the shock of being abruptly fired over a trumped-up charge within Countrywide wore off, I was more cocky than cautious. And an opportunity presented itself which seemed perfect.

I had met with Devon to learn about his Internet project and was very intrigued by what I learned. He and his two friends had built a prototype site with more than three thousand users, with a new version under construction that used a then cutting-edge Internet 2.0 software called Ruby on Rails. Their project was a reputation-building site for small local businesses called GoHuman.com. This site leveraged up-and-coming social media components to develop local marketplaces based on word-of-mouth marketing and reputation. Many of the ideas that would later gain traction in sites like Yelp, Angie's List, Groupon, and more were either built in or in the planning stages.

After a few meetings with the three young founders and their advisors, and a check from me for $30,000, I was named the cofounder of an exciting new Internet venture. Tomorrow it might rain, but I was betting on sunshine.

I loved the excitement of working with these bright young guys on GoHuman. com. They made up for their lack of business experience with energy, enthu-siasm, and creativity. I threw myself wholeheartedly into setting up a strategic plan and aggressively setting and pursuing targets and goals related to bringing "A World of Local Services" online.

Instant Karma

Time passes, but true love remains. The life of this world is, for the most part, nothing but a succession of illusions and deceptions. But true love is real, and the flames which fuel it burn forever, without beginning or end.

NIZAMI GANJAVI – "LEYLI AND MAJNUN"

The progress was dramatic at GoHuman. As the oldest member by far, and the primary investor, I drove the team hard, introducing a new level of business accountability to these recent college graduates, while also delineating roles and responsibilities. They were very open to the discipline I was introducing, excited by the momentum that was being built. I also orchestrated a number of meetings with other business professionals, who had experience with Internet ventures or at tech companies like Apple.

Before long, I was having discussions with senior business leaders about establishing a board and had engaged a franchise strategist, with whom I developed a fundraising and monetization model based on selling business services franchises based on the zip-code deployment of the GoHuman site.

JUNIOR'S FARM

The first few months of 2007 were intoxicating. The wedding date was getting closer, and my days were long and creative, as I worked to forge a shared spiritual vision—made more exciting by a synergy of very different perspectives. The Bahá'í views shared by my three young cofounders had been accepted since birth. My own insights, by contrast, were hard-fought—gleaned from an intense focus on using the Bible as lamp that lit my path throughout a very turbulent and eventful life.

The greatest sin in the Bahá'í Faith is the sin of backbiting. Bahá'ís are taught early and often to treat every other human being with the utmost respect. A Bahá'í worthy of the name will look beyond the faults and flaws of another person and work to bring out the positive. Certainly, they will never trash the reputation of another. The reputation-based features of GoHuman were based on the idea that this was a trait that non-Bahá'ís would also embrace, given half the chance.

Our emphasis was on cheery "help the provider make it right" features. Yelp, a site we had not heard of at the time, took the opposite path. They had a bit of a head start and gained quickly in popularity. With the benefit of hindsight, I realize Yelp's approach of empowering criticism was destined to catch on more quickly than the Bahá'í ideal of emphasizing the positive. At that time, however, a somewhat naïve desire to see the future arrive more quickly may have been a primary factor in our enthusiasm.

One of the most important concepts that—although not exclusive to Bahá'ís—is front and center in their thinking is the idea of local engagement. The administrative order of the Bahá'í Faith is democratic. There are no clergy in the Bahá'í faith—no ministers or priests, no individual spiritual leaders. Each local community is governed by an elected body of nine members, with bodies of nine governing at the national and international levels as well. None of the members of these bodies have any individual authority. Bahá'ís encourage individual initiative, and the only authority that exists comes from cooperation and consensus.

This principle is put into practice outside their faith through local grassroots involvement, engaging with interested parties on any number of positive topics related to their core values. The empowerment of local economies is in line with principles related to their idea of the establishment of the Kingdom of God on Earth. I was only beginning to understand the Bahá'í view of exactly how the Kingdom of God would arrive.

What appealed to me was the recognition of and commitment to (as the saying goes) being the change you wish to see in the world. Bahá'ís were, as a group, more aware of what this looked like than what I was used to seeing in religious believers. Rather than relying on future divine intervention, they were fully engaged with the world, seeking to align their current behavior with their vision of what the future society would be like. The allure of the supernatural was no substitute for digging deep to try to fix things now. Life should be devoted to understanding and at least trying to implement the principles by which God would transform the earth if or when He intervened.

Most striking to me in all this wasn't the similarity to the approach I had been chasing; rather, it was the difference. For starters, this was a ground-up versus top-down approach. The focus was on reaching consensus, not on obeying orders delivered by superiors. The most powerful difference of all was that their theology was grounded in inclusivity. For Bahá'ís, God was working with all humanity, through all religions. This was the polar opposite of the approach the WCG had taken—of a small, elite group with special access to God, in a world where everyone else was completely cut off from Him through disobedience. Humble submission to God and to authority was already ingrained in me, almost to a fault, but Bahá'ís helped me recognize my serious lack of humility and courtesy toward my fellow human beings. To a degree.

GoHuman.com was my primary outlet to attempt an integration of the unusual mix of old and new. On the one hand, it was there I could practice mirroring the impressive example of my partners. Inherent respect for each and every individual, no matter their religion, ethnicity, or social standing, was on display through their kindness and courtesy in day-to-day interactions between us and with others. On the other hand, my oversized spiritual ambition found an outlet in aggressive efforts to expand the vision of the project. My partners welcomed my recommendation to shift our focus from "A World of Local Services" to "Changing the Way the World Works." Why not try to build an alternative to Babylon the Great?

Empowering small, local businesses to compete with global multinationals was definitely a step in the right direction. While local mom and pop stores and franchise outlets were part of the global economy, they were directly connected to customers and workers and formed a more natural local ecosystem. Business transactions were likely to be more than just numbers through which operations and accounting departments manufactured riches for the owners and operators of gigantic corporations.

And while positive Bahá'í traits were rubbing off on me, this worked both ways, to a degree. As I became acquainted with what was going on "under the hood" of GoHuman.com, I saw that user activity on the site was nowhere near as robust as I had initially been led to believe. Devon acknowledged that GoHuman had been all but dead and that my arrival had resuscitated the company. He rolled up his sleeves to improve his accountability for measurable results, encouraging the other two partners to follow his example. To a degree. Why do I keep qualifying this? Because, although I was unaware of it at the time, my oversized ego was not rubbing off on them. It was rubbing them the wrong way.

SUN KING

In the meantime, though, having Bahá'í partners led to further engagement with the Bahá'í community in Los Angeles. Devon's involvement in music, in particular, led me to join him on several occasions at Bahá'í events, even without Angela. This exposure led to an increasingly genuine interest in the strange and surprising teachings of this new religion.

The aperture on a camera is the opening that allows light to enter. My religious perspective had previously been narrow and focused carefully on specific points, to peer through the darkness that surrounds us at a distant point of light. This was very effective in diving deeply into specific topics. The downside was that this was not an effective method at all in gaining a broad understanding.

Thankfully, cameras work very effectively at the other end of the spectrum as well. By shifting my focal point from a narrow to a broad one, I began arriving at satisfying answers to the questions I had with increasing persistence been pursuing from the opening pages of this trilogy. By adopting a very wide-angle lens and opening the aperture as far as I possibly could, I was letting in more light.

I had already opened the aperture to include a search for God through the revelation of creation. This was amplified by the Bahá'í belief in the oneness of religion and science. They also taught the essential unity of all religion, which I did not readily accept, but my general acceptance of them as a group of people encouraged the shift in focus to a macro lens. As light was entering my field of vision from a wide range of angles, a number of important items that had been hidden in choosing a narrow focus and applying numerous filters were suddenly illuminated.

Before we get into these, I want to make a key distinction between religion and revelation. Religion might be considered the organized interpretation and application of the revelation. But I believe history shows that religion becomes corrupt over time, as believers build upon erroneous interpretation. The remedy is to strip away the corruption and get back to the bedrock of the revelation.

When God hoisted the greater and lesser lights into the sky, He set them as our primary markers in the celestial road map, guiding humankind along its journey. The pattern of worship in the Mosaic covenant is provided by the moon that circles our planet, and this pattern of worship is laid out in the form of Israel's lunar calendar. Its high Holy Days are imbued with meaning through their historic and prophetic roots. In the Bible, waters are often symbolic of peoples, and like the tide responding to the moon, we are called to respond to the divine calendar, to circumambulate both its physical and spiritual mass.

The moon, however, does not generate any light or heat. In that way, it has a similarity to the tablets of stone, which Moses brought down from the mountain. The finger of God animated those tablets, in the same way the light of the sun animates the moon, providing the illumination that mapped out the pattern of worship for Israel. The people of Israel had asked that a veil be placed over Moses's face because he frightened, and perhaps blinded, them. Moses was providing illumination they were not ready for.

This pattern of worship points to Christ. He was the One they were not ready for, and when He arrived, the veil was stripped away. The moon guides us in darkness, but its light pales in the light of day, and it becomes scarcely visible in the light of the sun. To fail to update the understanding gained in the reflected light, and its shadows, once the clear light of the sun reveals the truth, was akin to being lost in a hall of mirrors at the fun house. There we look at reflections of reflections, or measure ourselves against a warped, corrupt version of ourselves. In such a situation we are unable to determine what our true reflection really is. And if we can't see ourselves as we truly are, it becomes impossible to actually crucify our egos. To see ourselves as we truly are, we must measure ourselves against Christ. We can't see Christ in ourselves, much less in others, when we are focused on a pattern of worship based on reflections, which Paul refers to as shadows.

While Jesus is clearly the intended aim of much of the Old Testament, this does not mean He, at His first coming, is the final end point. He, like Moses, pointed people forward to that which would come after Him. He stated quite clearly that there were things He could not yet tell His disciples and promised a future Comforter. He also promised to return, and it seems clear to me that only the Passover and Days of Unleavened Bread, the first third of the Holy Day cycle of the Jewish calendar, pointed to Christ's first coming, to the events related to the Israel of His day, and to the ascendancy of the religion that bears His name. Those that come later in the Jewish calendar year appear to relate to the global events described in the book of Revelation and elsewhere, written after His death, and which point forward from there, right down to our day.

The revelation of God is always moving forward, and humanity is always struggling in its efforts to see the light clearly and to ward off the always-encroaching darkness.

C MOON

The calendar which God had ordained for Israel, based on the governance of the greater and lesser lights discussed in the opening verses of the Bible, was subject to human observation. From this calendar's inception through the time of Jesus, the Jewish Talmud tells us the observance of the days ordained by the ruling lights was dependent on the observation of two witnesses. They would search for a visible crescent of a New Moon in the west (just after sunset). When they were able to see it, a New Moon would be declared.[1] Efforts to submit to the light, to circumambulate a spiritual mass, lead to insights at this intersection of religion, science, and human experience.

The role of free will is emphasized by this requirement to observe. It illustrates how humans, at the pinnacle of the physical creation, function as bridge particles of the spiritual plane of existence. Like the photons that are the communicators of light, bridging the gap between quantum mechanics and classical physics, we either have a positive or a negative spin on spiritual issues. Depending on which side of 3-D glasses someone is looking through, one or the other is filtered out. As observations cause the wave function in operation at the quantum level to collapse, resulting in a fixed decision, human ability to observe accurately, despite our bias, determines the structure that results from our decision. And that decision will depend on what hypothesis is used to test it—whether we are inclined to accept the possibility that there is a God or are disinclined to do so.

God will not force Himself on our consciousness, individually, or collectively. And we are not stuck in one position. Having free will enables us to switch back and forth from a negative to a positive orientation.[2]

We are in a womb today, and when Jesus says we will be born again, He really does mean that. Each of us will be born from this material existence into a spiritual one. How we decide to believe and act now, in this womb of physical existence, in this nursery called earth, will determine whether we have developed the virtues needed to accomplish and excel in the next world. You might say that if we fail to develop virtues we will be born handicapped, in some way or another. And at the human level, the free will given to us at creation enables the binary distinction between what is a goat or a sheep in God's eyes.[3] This is ultimately what determines our experience in the next world, regardless of what we believe. What distinguishes isn't what one believes but what one does.

---

1 John D. Keyser, "*Crescent vs. Astronomical New Moon*," Hope of Israel Ministries, accessed May 10, 2018, http://www.hope-of-israel.org/crescentmoon.html.

2 Interestingly, recent theories being advanced on how gravity emerges have similarities to what I am attempting to describe here. See Anil Ananthaswamy, "*Gravity May Be Created by Strange Flashes in the Quantum Realm*," New Scientist, September 20, 2017, https://www.newscientist.com/article/mg23531444-600-spontaneous-collapses-may-show-how-to-unite-quantum-theory-and-gravity/.

3 Matthew 25:31-32: "When the Son of man shall come in his glory, and all the holy angels with him, then shall he sit upon the throne of his glory: and before him shall be gathered all nations: and he shall separate them one from another, as a shepherd divideth his sheep from the goats."

When a person decides not to help his or her fellow human in need, the Holy Spirit is quenched, and he or she becomes a goat. But what does that mean? In this context it might be helpful to understand a goat as also being the proverbial blind man, groping around in a cave, while thinking he can see.[4] The law can tutor us, as the apostle Paul explains in Galatians 3:23-24, it can guide us toward the light, but often we're not enlightened by it. That requires faith, which I believe is understanding—and the kind of trust in God that helps us, through our obedience, to recognize the difference between darkness and light.

Christ transcended evil by willingly giving Himself up as a sacrifice. He came to save us from ourselves, not from some outside enemy. He told His servants not to fight, but to take up their own crosses.

The temptation must be resisted, however, to judge the descendants of Jacob, who for thousands of years have been following the Mosaic covenant, the tutor. They have arrived the hard way at the understanding granted from following that tutor, following ordinances about what to eat or not eat, what to do or not to do, and when to do and not to do it.

God clearly wanted them to understand the spiritual nature of their covenant, as these explicit, detailed instructions created a people, over thousands of years, with a shared culture and a history of having emerged from slavery. This gave them the strength and vision to survive systematic persecution, even multiple attempts at genocide. Christ was a Jew, and I believe this is a tie-in to the otherwise somewhat difficult statement that He learned through suffering.[5]

In any case, whether or not they accepted Him, the symbol of the cross was laid upon them very heavily. They too were persecuted as much for their righteousness as for anything else. Their adherence to their laws and the Sign of their covenant made it easy to identify them and also gave the church that claimed the symbol of the cross a reason to become a major contributor to and a participant in that persecution. The persecution of the Jews also serves, generally, as a valuable lesson for humankind.

That Israel is at the center of biblical prophecy was no mystery, but somehow I had missed the enormous significance of Israel holding fast to the Sign which gave them their identity. That identity, on the negative side, enabled the application of the yellow star in Nazi Germany. The positive aspect of that identity included very specific physical promises to the tribes of Israel, under

4 Deuteronomy 28:29 and Isaiah 59:10 refer to this, but I'm referring to Plato's A of the Cave, in which the cave dwellers live in the dark, with their whole experience being based on shadowy images cast by the light they never really experience.
5 Hebrews 5:7-9: "Who, in the days of His flesh, when He had offered up prayers and supplications, with vehement cries and tears to Him who was able to save Him from death, and was heard because of His godly fear, though He was a Son, yet He learned obedience by the things which He suffered. And having been perfected, He became the author of eternal salvation to all who obey Him" (NKJV).

their covenant, that were never intended for Christians. By realizing that I was not, nor had ever been, specifically under the Mosaic covenant, I began to see more clearly the role that those who were, in fact, under it were playing in God's great plan for humankind.

BACKWARDS TRAVELLER

I opened this chapter with a quote taken from an epic love story by a Persian poet, "The Story of Layla and Majnun" by Nizami Ganjavi. I learned about this story from my new Bahá'í friends, for whom it symbolized a passionate search for God. This spiritual interpretation may very well be unique to Bahá'ís, as the average person relates much more readily to the doomed love story inherent in it.

The story caught my interest because it answered the music-geek question of why Eric Clapton chose "Layla" as the title of the song dedicated to his ill-fated obsession with George Harrison's wife, the unattainable woman. And unlike Majnun, my supposedly insane desire for an unobtainable woman, Angela, had resulted in a lengthy engagement, which would soon reach its long-awaited conclusion. But it was the Bahá'í understanding of this metaphor that began to occupy my thoughts.

The spiritual implication of Majnun's desire is described in the Bahá'í book *The Seven Valleys*: "It is related that one day they came upon Majnun sifting the dust, and his tears flowing down. They said, 'What doest thou?' He said, 'I seek for Layli.' They cried, 'Alas for thee! Layli is of pure spirit, and thou seekest her in the dust!' He said, 'I seek her everywhere; haply somewhere I shall find her.'"[6] I came to realize I had spent decades searching for God in ancient texts, typified by the Dead Sea Scrolls.

These scrolls predate Christ by a few years but are records of much earlier documents, lost and long since disintegrated. This brought my particular madness, my obsessive search for God, into stark relief. Like Majnun, I was searching in the dust. And yet my passion was more vibrant than ever. Without abandoning my trust in these ancient manuscripts, my search was widening out beyond them. And I was making swift progress.

The excitement was also building at GoHuman.com, as version 2.0 was launched. The design was inviting, the interface was intuitive to users, and it had a dashboard that allowed us to track enrollments and use of the site. We enthusiastically began a daily analysis of the results of our marketing efforts, even as I was reanalyzing everything I knew about God and the Bible in light of a steady stream of new religious inputs. That reevaluation helped

---

6 Bahá'u'lláh, *The Seven Valleys and the Four Valleys*, (US *Bahá'í* Publishing Trust, 1991 pocket-size edition), 65.

me further reassess the path I had so diligently followed for decades, and the one I was on now.

My experience at Countrywide, for example, had reawakened my awareness and increased my understanding that the planet was under the dominion of Babylon the Great. We, as a species, had entered the era described by Revelation 18. How is it that people following good intentions so often became participants in such horrible outcomes?

Unexpected outcomes are, generally speaking, just areas of science we don't yet understand. The elements and factors are more interrelated and complex, and the laws are more subtle and flexible than our minds can comprehend. In the area of gravity, for example, the latest unified string theory that includes gravity is better understood in terms of geometry than anything else—the complex patterns that give structure to our existence are more beautiful and perfect than we can imagine.[7]

A reevaluation of Newton, one of the fathers of physics, has uncovered that he spent decades experimenting with alchemy.[8] The theory is that he was searching for a way to understand the strange, unseen, and seemingly unscientific nature of gravity. Einstein's description of quantum mechanics as "spooky action at a distance" comes to mind. Einstein got his answer by reflecting on the moon and the tide. He pondered over how gravity could travel faster than light, in that the moon's pull on the tide was felt before its light hit the earth. This led to his crowning achievement, the General Theory of Relativity, and the understanding that mass bent space-time.[9]

Regardless of whether we fully understand the subtle forces of nature, it is still correct to describe them as dependable, even if incredibly complex, frameworks of laws. I view the advancement of our understanding and harnessing of these in the light of Isaiah 42:21. As humanity advances natural laws are being magnified and made honorable—able to be more fully obeyed, as in when we "honor a commitment."[10] My exposure to the Bahá'í faith's emphasis on the essential unity of science and religion, as well as learning from the history of the Catholic Church's battle with Galileo, helped me understand that trying to force science into a theological mold is doomed to failure. There is nothing in the Bible that insists God didn't create by creating

7 Natalie Wolchover, "*Physicists Discover Geometry Underlying Particle Physics,*" Quanta Magazine, September 17, 2013, accessed June 28, 2018, https://www.quantamagazine.org/physicists-discover-geometry-underlying-particle-physics-20130917/.

8 "*Isaac Newton,*" Alchemy Lab, accessed June 28, 2018, https://www.alchemylab.com/isaac_newton.htm.

9 "*Einstein and Curving Spacetime,*" Wild Maths, accessed June 28, 2018, https://wild.maths.org/einstein-and-curving-spacetime.

10 Isaiah 42:21: "The Lord is well pleased for his righteousness' sake; he will magnify the law, and make it honourable."

forces at work behind an evolutionary process. But the reverse is equally true. For science to deny the possibility of God is a bias that has no place in science.

Both Newton and Einstein comingled the two. In Newton's case, it has recently been uncovered that he studied the Bible intensively, creating timelines predicting the end of all things might occur in 2060.[11] His theological ideas, including his rejection of the Trinity, were kept secret due to the power of the Church of England at that time. In the case of Einstein, several famous quotes, such as "I want to know God's thoughts," illustrate his interest in God.

I had long believed that God refuses to allow Himself to be found by skeptics, but increasingly believed that He allows Himself to be found by the sincere. Now, it appears, even the brightest and most confirmed atheists and agnostics will find out one day that the only way to move forward, scientifically, is through a spiritual understanding of God. To illustrate this, we must travel back in time and visit Göbekli Tepe, using a *National Geographic* article titled "The Birth of Religion."[12]

The massive stone pillars of Göbekli Tepe in southern Turkey are arranged in circular patterns reminiscent of Stonehenge. But while Stonehenge is considered prehistoric, it is positively modern compared to these temples erected some eight thousand years prior to Stonehenge and the Pyramids of Giza. When these sites were established, humans were hunter-gatherers. Agriculture had not yet been adopted, and huts were the prevalent forms of architecture. This makes the fact that the pillars of Göbekli Tepe are hewn and carved—decorated with bas-reliefs of animals, including snakes, wild boars, gazelles, and scorpions—all the more astounding.

The article lays out the reason why archaeologists, paleontologists, and other -ologists declare Göbekli Tepe to be a complete game changer. "Archaeologists are still excavating Göbekli Tepe and debating its meaning. What they do know is that the site is the most significant in a volley of unexpected findings that have overturned earlier ideas about our species' deep past." Excavator Klaus Schmidt explains, "First came the temple, then the city."[13] This simple statement turns everything modern science thought it knew about the origin of civilization and religion on its head.

The belief that the revolution of evolution that occurred in the Neolithic Period was due to environmental factors and the discovery of agriculture is being replaced by something else entirely. Göbekli Tepe indicates that the catalyst that drove humanity aggressively forward in understanding and abilities was the

---

11 Stephen D. Stobolen, "Statement on the Date 2060," Isaac Newton: Theology, Prophecy, Science and Religion (blog), last revised June, 2003, accessed June 28, 2018, https://isaac-newton.org/statement-on-the-date-2060/
12 Charles C. Mann, "The Birth of Religion," *National Geographic,* June 2011, 34-59.
13 Ibid.

introduction of religious ideas. But what really caught my interest when I came across this article were the patterns of worship indicated by the installations.

C'MON PEOPLE / COSMICALLY CONSCIOUS

Earlier I mentioned that certain events in India had emerged as a turning point for me. My trip had unexpectedly turned into a tour of off-the-grid India, in which I had baptized two men in an outdoor pool in a public park. The entrance of the park was guarded by the giant statue of a hooded cobra, and after we exited the park, the car in which we were traveling had broken down. I spent a miserable night trying to sleep on the dirty cement of an outdoor garage in the nearby town of Tiruvannemalai, where attempts were being made to repair the car. My misery was compounded by the fear of getting sick from the pool water in which I had baptized the two men or the mosquitoes that were, among other things, preventing sleep. The low point came when, in the middle of the night, we were overwhelmed by the commotion of noisy worshipers in motion, flowing around us on both sides. These believers were honoring their god by circumambulating the mountain at whose base we happened to be camping.

At the time, I was thinking how deceived they all were, but increasingly I was able to pinpoint that moment as the beginning of a spiritual awakening that was more and more granting me answers to all the questions that had plagued my adult life. It was like the walls of Jericho falling—the strongholds of religious fantasy and superstition which had kept me from improving my understanding of God and His will.

The biblical story has Israel, under Joshua's direction, circling around Jericho for seven days to bring down the fortress walls of that stronghold. My original irritation at the word "circumambulation" had been a negative feedback loop which caused reflection on the alternate word, "orbit." This in turn had opened up a connection between this spiritual pattern of worship and the basic building blocks of the universe. And it reinforced the idea that there might be more than meets the eye behind God choosing this method to destroy Jericho.

The fractal patterns represented by quantum particle behavior, once the wave function collapses and they become dependable, versus only probabilities, aggregate up into fixed relationships between particles. Quantum entanglement is a likely suspect in how these, in turn, continue a pattern of circling around a center of mass, thus aggregating up into atoms and molecules. This is predicated on laws related to orbits. These particles could be said to circumambulate around each other. As the aggregation continues, greater mass and attraction are created, leading to greater aggregation. Eventually, the complexity increases, and greater potentialities unfold. The aggregation of these orbits, and the patterns and potentialities, eventually lead to life and human beings and consciousness.

As we extend our own consciousness, through our powers of observation, out beyond our earth, we find we are on a small round rock, with a smaller rock orbiting us, as we circle around a massive burning orb, which is actually a rather smallish star. The sun is the central mass of a modest solar system, circling some other point in what we have labeled the Milky Way. From our vantage point, the Milky Way appears as a band because the disk-shaped structure of what is actually a spiral galaxy is viewed from within. Until the 1920s, most astronomers thought the Milky Way contained all the stars in the universe.

Edwin Hubble's observations showed that it was just one of many galaxies, even though it is estimated to contain from one hundred to four hundred billion stars and three trillion planets, all orbiting its center of mass.[14] Recent estimates on the number of galaxies in the observable universe range from two hundred billion to two trillion, gravitationally organized, orbiting around each other in groups, clusters, and superclusters. We do not yet fully understand this vast mosaic, although science continues to push the boundaries of our current understanding as it explores the material that comprises the universe and their relational orbits.

WATCHING THE WHEELS

The discovery of Göbekli Tepe brought all this into stark relief for me, underlining the fact that circumambulation is a method of opening up the spiritual understanding of all things. Prior to establishing any form of civilization, it seems our ancestors first established centers of spiritual mass around which they circled, forming a fractal pattern which permeated subsequent religions and systems of human organization.

In considering the history of systems of human organization, the city of Bab El immediately came to mind. At the time what was orbing in my head was a sensed connection between the Tower of Babel and Babylon the Great, the global economic system which was trading in every known precious commodity, including the bodies and souls of people. This was partially due to my introduction to the man known as the Báb—the Gate—and his connection to the

---

14 Brian Done, "Milky Way Galaxy Atlas," Accessed June 29, 2018, http://www.milkywaygalaxyatlas.com/.

source of Babylon, while appearing at the moment of its end-time fulfillment. The idea of circumambulation in evidence at Göbekli Tepe was also important. There was more, much more, behind the story of the Tower of Babel, which I was struggling to uncover. There were a few more circles I had to walk in relative darkness before the light of awareness would fully dawn.

As I believe occurs for those who practice circumambulation, our awareness and understanding can improve as we recognize the true reality of our own place within the cosmos. Each of us, otherwise, views ourselves at the center of our own little universe. Scientific expressions of the nature of the universe, from its initial seconds to how the observable universe functions, through the expansion phase, in which space-time is fundamentally altered as the system of systems expands beyond observable limits, confirm this.[15] I'll circle back and explain this shortly.

Einstein's formulation of absolute space-time can be understood by viewing it, in its entirety, as a loaf of bread. Individual observers might slice it up at different angles, depending on location and movement, but when the slices are reassembled the loaf hasn't changed, and it is still the same for everybody. This is helpful in making a point about understanding our place in a greater reality. Our free will–based perception is important, but to align with spiritual reality we need to reduce the influence of our ego thinking over our perception. Circumambulating around a point other than ourselves, realizing we orbit a spiritual center, rather than the other way around, is helpful in achieving this.

In this context, I have to share two of my favorite jokes.

How many prima donnas does it take to change a light bulb? Just one. She holds it while the world revolves around her.

This was a reality I was familiar with and aware of. But awareness alone isn't enough.

How many psychologists does it take to change a light bulb? Just one. But the light bulb has to really want *to change.*

As I became aware of what I needed to change, my desire to do so increased rapidly. It may well be true, as John Lennon sang, that we all shine on, like

---

15 The Hardness of the Heart covers my initial exploration of these themes. Subsequent scientific discovery confirms and extends what I outlined in that prior volume. This article is a good place to start for those who wish to dive deeper: Physics Stack Exchange, https://physics.stackexchange.com/questions/123875/does-everything-orbit-around-some-universal-center-of-mass.

the moon and the stars and the sun. But a personal Copernican Revolution is needed, in which we realize we are not the center of the universe.

Years earlier I had realized that my spiritual standing with God depended on my treatment of my brothers and sisters. What had changed was a deeper understanding that I was no different from them. This realization was a further "circumcision of my heart," to use the language of the Christian covenant. Circumcision is, in this context, one more example of the power of circumambulation. This tiny fractal pattern, a circular incision, is woven into the fabric of religious history. It was the Sign of the Abrahamic covenant, and he was the father of monotheistic religion. It appears to symbolize how the barriers and veils that separate us from God are removed by this practice of circumambulating around the walls and strongholds. This ritual brings down barriers and creates purity.

My prior experiences had created my own personal circumambulation around the centers of mass that I honored. But any and all baggage from that experience was affecting my trajectory and limited God's ability to further reveal Himself, even as my desire to know Him better was increasing. Humility and detachment led to a renewed flow of insight, a positive feedback loop that helped me tighten my orbit around God.

Let 'Em In

But, instead of what our imagination makes us suppose and which we worthless try to discover, life gives us something that we could hardly imagine.
— MARCEL PROUST

By shedding the weight of things that had been important to me, I found there was less to drag me away from the center of mass I wanted to attain. This was how God was able to help me draw closer to Him.

Mark Twain's famous prediction came to mind in this context. "I came in with Halley's Comet in 1835. It is coming again next year, and I expect to go out with it. It will be the greatest disappointment of my life if I don't go out with Halley's Comet. The Almighty has said, no doubt: 'Now here are these two unaccountable freaks; they came in together, they must go out together.'" Samuel Clemens was indeed born in 1835 just after Halley's Comet appeared, and the day after its brightest appearance, in 1910, he died of a heart attack.

ALL THOSE YEARS AGO

Childhood events had damaged my self-esteem, and I later compensated by embracing an oversized belief in my destiny, in the light of God's love and plan for me. This set me off on an eccentric orbit, like a comet. I would circle in close to the sun, before my momentum and trajectory sent me back out into distant, dark space. Dramatic, exotic, and sometimes bizarre and dangerous experiences provided feedback on my way back in for another close encounter with the source of light.

My focus on God and His Word and events which brought my ego under control provided feedback loops which began to regulate that orbit. One of the biggest of these trajectory changes was letting go of the idea that I was part of a special covenant God made with Israel four thousand years ago. A new, more mature spiritual footing allowed me to better address the question about exactly where I fit in within God's plan.

Our local example of creation, our solar system, is exhibit A in God's educational program related to our place in that plan. The Genesis discussion of the greater and lesser lights, the sun and moon, and how they generate calendars, days, seasons, and time itself, was God's revelation to us in our infancy. As history progressed, the struggle between the Catholic Church and Copernicus and Galileo about whether we are at the center of the solar system illustrated how even that local revelation forced us to address the tension between religion and science and introduced the challenges of subjectivity and objectivity. The development of science provided visibility into similar systems within creation at micro and macro levels, and everything in between. All of this was unimaginable to our ancestors, even as it provides amazing opportunities for us to grow in our understanding and appreciation of God's greatness.

Just under one hundred years ago, we began using quartz clocks to measure time. Quartz has the property of producing very reliable electric pulsations. Two billion quartz clocks are produced each year, used in everything from oven timers to pacemakers. Since they are affected by temperature and pressure changes over time, we rely on what are known as atomic clocks to accurately measure time at a micro level.

Atomic clocks are constructed by a combined measurement relying on the orbits of electrons in quartz and Cesium 133. These so-called oscillations or waves per second, defined as movement back and forth, are expressed with the term hertz (written "Hz"). The 32,768 Hz of a quartz clock and the 9,192,631,770 Hz of a Cesium 133 atom are integrated in this device. This system of systems incorporates a self-adjusting feedback loop, and in many ways it's like a mini solar system. It is said that if the most accurate atomic clock that exists today had been running since the big bang, it would be less than a second off.[1]

And speaking of the big bang, let's discuss time at the macro level. Mechanisms which incorporate the largest systems known to us in tracking time are known as astronomical clocks. They are thought to have originated in eleventh century China and were improved upon in thirteenth century Europe. Interest

---

1 Alex Klokus, "World's Most Accurate Clock Loses Just 1 Second Every 16 Billion Years," Futurism, March 2, 2015, https://futurism.com/worlds-most-accurate-clock-loses-just-1-second-every-16-billion-years/.

in such devices was revived in the eighteenth century. The key point in this discussion is that, over time, they moved from merely calculating days, times, and seasons, based on our solar system, to include much larger cycles that incorporated the zodiac.[2]

The key takeaway is that our little daily, weekly, and monthly cycles are merely blips in a much larger clock that incorporates constellations of stars, as outlined in the first few verses of Genesis.[3] Its reference to stars, which at first glance almost appears to be an afterthought, has emerged over time as an indicator of sequential epochs in civilization. In this context it's an important calibration in a vast prophetic framework, laid out in intricate detail. On the one hand, God's fingerprint is infused in every particle, across time and space. On the other hand, God's signature is recorded in every letter in the weave that spreads across the sixty-six books of the Bible, which were remembered and then recorded over many thousands of years.

Which is utterly mind-blowing in its scope and perfection.

IN MY LIFE

The promise of James 1:17 had often reassured me that no matter how bad things seemed, my heavenly Father would make it all turn out right:

Every good gift and every perfect gift is from above, and cometh down from the Father of lights, with whom there is no variableness, neither shadow of turning.

As my understanding of the nature of God's physical revelation increased, the words "Father of lights" and "no variableness, neither shadow of turning" brought to mind both atomic and astronomical clocks. And brought to mind that all His promises were part of an exact prophetic calendar more accurate than anything humans could devise.

The fractal patterns of physics start with the anomalies of quantum mechanics, but nonetheless aggregate up at the molecular level into those mini solar systems and galaxies called atoms and molecules. All of these aggregate

---

2 Wikipedia, s.v. "Astronomical Clock," last updated April 24, 2018, https://en.wikipedia.org/wiki/Astronomical_clock.

3 Genesis 1:14-16: "And God said, 'Let there be lights in the expanse of the heavens to separate the day from the night. And let them be for signs and for seasons, and for days and years, and let them be lights in the expanse of the heavens to give light upon the earth.' And it was so. And God made the two great lights—the greater light to rule the day and the lesser light to rule the night—and the stars" (ESV).

up to what David exclaimed to be the heavens that declare the glory of God.[4] All the forces that enable mass and gravity, along with the bodies and orbital patterns they generate create the vast stellar light show that exists to declare His glory. His written revelation is the key to unlock the message of the cosmos— that which it is declaring, prophetic perfection, immaculately measured by all the mass and energy in the universe, calibrated to within microseconds from a geocentric perspective.

Einstein, the father of much of the understanding inherent in the science I've addressed above, is well known for having said, "I want to know God's thoughts—the rest are mere details." To know God's thoughts, one must be open-minded enough to allow His revelation to enter. Einstein also recognized that "Science without religion is lame; religion without science is blind." Most of us are inclined to reject one in favor of the other. Meeting the Bahá'ís had reinforced my hard-won belief that in order to grow we needed both.

Prophecy outlined that what had started with Nimrod, at the original Babylon, with humanity's desire to make a name for itself and build a tower to heaven, would evolve as a concept, and in the end times, become Babylon the Great. The latter is the global, materialistic system, driven by greed and a lust for power and control over others and the entire planet, with corrupt religion as an integrated component. Having so recently gained an insider's view of how the global economy worked, I was more convinced than ever that we were at that point in the unfolding of space-time.

My enthusiasm for GoHuman.com was fueled by the idea that we were building an integrated online marketplace that would provide an alternative to Babylon the Great. GoHuman was a platform to enable a collaborative network of small businesses and consumers, connecting owners and customers at the human, local community level. The audacity of this might seem strange, but the growth of Google, Facebook and Amazon.com illustrate that it was theoretically possible and, at the time, believable.

Thoughts were swirling around in my head, as the possibility of an entirely new level of understanding about God and the nature of our relationship to Him and the creation was opening up. My efforts to align scientific research on particle physics and stellar bodies with books claiming to contain revelation was all in an effort to gain clarity on my own existence. While I was no Mark Twain, this ambition is of the same kind that drove him to compare himself to Halley's Comet. It's also no different from that which causes people to consult and reflect on their horoscope, looking for insight or inspiration from the heavens.

---

4 Psalm 19:1-3 (which Paul reiterates in Romans 1:20): "The heavens declare the glory of God; and the firmament shows His handiwork. Day unto day utters speech, and night unto night reveals knowledge. There is no speech nor language where their voice is not heard" (NKJV).

We are created from the elements of the earth, the dust of the ground. The earth originated in the stars, and it is accurate to say, as did Joni Mitchell in her song "Woodstock", that we are stardust. Our bodies, composed of this dust, are, at an even more fundamental level, a delicate balance of forces woven at the quantum level and aggregated up from there.

At the human consciousness level, our free will allows an aggregation of tiny, binary choices that create the fractal patterns that enable us to master, to conquer the universe in which we live. And we desire and strive to achieve beyond the station we were assigned. We are anchored to earth, while reaching for the stars, the source of our origin.

Everything on this dustspeck called earth is dependent on its orbit around the sun. All of this is held in intricate balance by a myriad of forces that keep everything from flying apart into total chaos. And, for our spiritual selves, it is a delicate balance to become "centered" and achieve alignment with our Creator rather than become "wandering stars."[5]

In terms of relative size, we are at the center of the universe, the midpoint, in orders of magnitude, between those quantum particles and the largest galaxies. In terms of composition, we are mostly space. Our actual particle components are held in orbits that look very much like the orbits we see at the macro scale. And we occupy the space at the center of size between the micro and macro universe. Since, in this sense, we each, literally, occupy the center of our own universe, it isn't surprising that we struggle to overcome self-centered thought and behavior.

I was trying to create a space for myself as well. One within which I could comfortably fit. And my efforts to understand the cosmos, the history of our species, science, religion, and everything in between, would not have been possible without the grounding that my relationship with Angela was giving me.

YOU GAVE ME THE ANSWER

Angela had expanded her circle of Bahá'í friends to include two lovely ladies. Rahel was a tall blonde working in the film industry in the Los Angeles area and could easily have been mistaken for a model. Her friend Aden was

---

5 Jude 11-13: "Woe unto them! for they have gone in the way of Cain, and ran greedily after the error of Balaam for reward, and perished in the gainsaying of Core. These are spots in your feasts of charity, when they feast with you, feeding themselves without fear: clouds they are without water, carried about of winds; trees whose fruit withereth, without fruit, twice dead, plucked up by the roots; raging waves of the sea, foaming out their own shame; wandering stars, to whom is reserved the blackness of darkness for ever."

from Ethiopia and was the opposite of Rahel in color and stature but equally attractive as a person and in spirit.

They offered to help Angela and me better understand the essential equality of all religions, a topic which, not surprisingly, given my background, I was struggling with. They offered to meet with us weekly to read a Bahá'í book titled *One Common Faith*. This book was commissioned by and prepared under the supervision of the highest administrative body of the Bahá'í faith, the Universal House of Justice.

Meeting once a week to read this book was fascinating and delightful. The experience of studying and discussing a well-researched and extremely well-written treatise with three amazingly beautiful and grace-filled women was transformational.

The book is but fifty-six slightly oversized and densely written pages, but it took us the better part of Angela's and my thirteen-month engagement to get through it. This was due to the approach of reading and discussing one para-graph at a time, coupled with the fact that I didn't leave any stone unturned in my examination of its premise. I was determined to compare each and every word against my understanding of the Bible as the Word of God, whether they liked it or not. I was challenging both the facts and the narrative, while also testing and observing the reactions of the people who believed them.

Rahel and Aden surely had their patience tried. They admitted they had never experienced this degree of examination and analysis. They were chal-lenged by some of what I said, but never once did they become impatient or dismissive of my pushing and pulling at the material. On the contrary, they proved to my satisfaction that the Bahá'í profession of acceptance of other religions was not mere lip service. Never once did they react negatively. They welcomed the bulk of what I introduced from the Bible, though much of it was coming from a very foreign place for them.

Many Bahá'ís tend to view the Bible as symbolic, and I was a fundamen-talist. But they seemed quite interested in the discussions that I admittedly at times dominated. In short, they passed my ongoing and seemingly never-ending tests with flying colors.

My view of women was, in general, conflicted. This stemmed from expe-riences that began in the womb of a chain-smoking, alcoholic mother. While I had loved her dearly, my mother's failure to nurture, protect, and teach had produced serious negative consequences for me. The example of these three very different women was as important as what we read in *One Common Faith*.

These months of intimate study of God's Word with them helped change my attitude toward women in general. This gradual but profound shift flowed naturally from having settled my concerns on what the Bible taught about the equality of men and women. The gentle washing of deeply rooted negative attitudes about women may have contributed to a gradual acceptance of a commonality across all religions.

Would God really have allowed the majority of the planet to fester for millennia under a global deception without offering the kind of assistance He had offered Israel? It made more sense to believe that God's decision to create the racial, cultural, and linguistic separation after Babel required Him to send servants, teachers, prophets, and apostles at different times to different geographies, peoples, and cultures. And none of the resulting religions passed the test of doctrinal or behavioral purity needed to prove others to be, by comparison, a satanic counterfeit.

It would likely bore most readers to outline a point-by-point reexamination of Bible passages I thought supported my previous understanding, some of which has already been done in the previous volume, so I'll just state that this electron switched from a negative to a positive spin on this point. Relevant verses no longer seemed to dogmatically, or in detail, say what I had previously interpreted them as saying. Verses which seemed to say the opposite grew in importance. A simple example of this are Jesus's statements about those not with Him being against Him, while also saying the opposite.[6]

The study circle with Aden and Rahel and my engagement to Angela took place parallel with my fall from grace at Countrywide and the launch of GoHuman.com. One memorable highlight was an engagement party, at which I surprised Angela with a beautiful diamond and platinum ring. That evening, with the love and joy present at the party, attended by old and new friends, all celebrating an exhilarating high point on an amazing journey, exceeded the excitement of just about any of my prior experiences.

It seemed like every week brought more joy and light into my life. One example was Paith's wedding. Paith held a special place in Angela's heart due to having introduced her to the Bahá'í faith. She was also an amazing example of the radiant essence every Bahá'í we met seemed to possess. Her wedding took place in Portland, Oregon, during the Christmas holiday season, which Angela and I spent with her family in Milwaukee, Wisconsin. We managed to arrange a rather grueling flight schedule that could accommodate a layover of several hours in Portland, allowing us to arrive just before the ceremony and stay for most of the wedding festivities before returning to the airport.

---

6 Mark 9:40: "For he that is not against us is on our part." And Luke 9:50: "And Jesus said unto him, Forbid him not: for he that is not against us is for us."

The free and joyful spirit and the obvious warmth of the entire wedding party and all the guests contrasted sharply with the celebration of a holiday I had always considered pagan. However wonderful Angela's family was, Christmas is burdened by ostensibly being a celebration of Christ's birth while being built on misrepresentations. Christ was not actually born at that time of year, so its alignment with the equinox is out of alignment with divine signs, days, times, and seasons set at creation. The crass materialism that fuels it is papered over by silly fantasies about Santa, the North Pole, and elves.

The wedding, on the other hand, was a simply elegant event. The decorations and food were generous wedding gifts from loving family and friends, and the toasts and activities were spontaneous gifts full of heart and poetry. The only formal ceremony came when the bride and groom proclaimed to each other the simple vow "We will all verily abide by the Will of God."

I was stunned. Floored. Entranced.

DON'T BE CARELESS LOVE

This vow rang true on so many levels. And it reinforced the deep spiritual bond Angela and I felt for each other. We determined to pattern our ceremony around the Bahá'í example.

While working with Devon and his partners in launching GoHuman.com my interactions with many different Bahá'ís in many different circumstances and situations continued to increase. This was both wonderful and a bit disturbing. Paith, her new husband, Rahel, Aden, Devon, and all the others, without exception, had the attitudes about God, religion, spirituality—and the application of these attitudes—that I had been striving to achieve throughout the long and winding road I had traveled my entire life.

How could this be? How could these people be so much more in alignment with searching out the message of the Bible and the God behind it than those who professed to follow it?

Yes, they claimed acceptance of Abraham, Moses, and Christ, but they had this strange idea that more recent manifestations of God had revealed new things. They were engaged in attempting to transform the world using the principles and teachings brought by religion throughout history but filtered through these new manifestations. This was very different from my understanding of the Bible, which had Christ actively and visibly assuming control of the planet upon His return, with an army of spirit beings at His side.

I could accept that their intentions were pure and admire the nature of what they were doing. But I could not accept that Christ had already returned and that the Bahá'í Faith was all that His return had accomplished.

Despite my reservations, I had no concerns about my acceptance of these people; their sincerity and their actions were that striking. This was made easier by their unconditional acceptance of me, exceeding by far the stingy respect of others that my prior belief system had only grudgingly offered. It was a growth opportunity for me to reciprocate what they offered. So I tried to apply that famous Yoga greeting, "Namaste" ("the Spirit in me acknowledges the Spirit in you"), without judging anyone's religious beliefs. After all, I had been asking God to help me focus on the identifying Sign of the Christian covenant—pure, unconditional, unqualified love. The kind that is indiscriminate and easily recognized by all.[7]

And in aligning with this Sign in my interactions with and opinions about the people I was meeting in this strange religion something quite astounding happened. As bizarre and inexplicable as it might seem, regardless of what I still considered to be obvious errors in their prophetic interpretation, I came to recognize that these people, more than any other group I had met, fulfilled the Sign of the Christian covenant.

As an independent, third-party observer, I had to admit that, in practice and in the beliefs that supported them, Bahá'ís loved not only Bahá'ís, but everyone else as well. They had a genuine, heartfelt, unconditional love of humankind. It was a core component of their spiritual DNA, and they were selflessly, and without hope of gain, putting this love into practice.

Though Bahá'ís would never explicitly claim to be following Christ to the exclusion of Moses, Buddha, or Bahá'u'lláh, as Christians would generally demand, it was implicit in their theology. Christ commanded us to follow Him, and the teachings of the Bahá'í Faith enabled them to appear almost effortless in doing so. They held all people to be the same and thus exemplified the mind of Christ.[8]

I had tested them, and they showed that they were sincerely applying this principle. Whenever push came to shove, as it did in my exploration of a variety of subjects, it was my understanding of what Christ taught that changed, upon closer comparison, not the teachings of their faith. And the more I openly investigated those teachings, the more amazed I became.

---

7 John 13:35: "By this shall all men know that ye are my disciples, if ye have love one to another."

8 Philippians 2:3-5: "Let nothing be done through strife or vainglory; but in lowliness of mind let each esteem other better than themselves. Look not every man on his own things, but every man also on the things of others. Let this mind be in you, which was also in Christ Jesus."

A quote from a man they called "the Master"—'Abdu'l-Bahá—the son of the founder of their faith, is a good example of this:

If a small number of people gather lovingly together, with absolute purity and sanctity, with their hearts free of the world, experiencing the emotions of the Kingdom and the powerful magnetic forces of the Divine, and being at one in their happy fellowship, that gathering will exert its influence over all the earth.[9]

GIMME SOME TRUTH

My expectation of Christ's return had always been based on the earth-shaking events described by the Hebrew prophets and the book of Revelation. And yet, in explaining how it would unfold, He had used examples that were much more organic. The twin parables of a mustard seed and leaven, for example, in Luke 13:18-21:

Then said he, Unto what is the kingdom of God like? and whereunto shall I resemble it? It is like a grain of mustard seed, which a man took, and cast into his garden; and it grew, and waxed a great tree; and the fowls of the air lodged in the branches of it. And again he said, Whereunto shall I liken the kingdom of God? It is like leaven, which a woman took and hid in three measures of meal, till the whole was leavened.

What 'Abdu'l-Bahá wrote seemed to be right in line with these parables. And of particular interest to me was a reference to the "powerful magnetic forces of the Divine," as this gathering exerted its influence over all the earth. The Bahá'ís were absolutely beginning to exert their influence over me, both in terms of the warmth of their pure embrace and in how their teachings were fueling my intellectual quest for coherence.

An oversimplified answer to the question "How does magnetism occur?" would be to state that electrons create magnetic fields as they orbit around their atomic nuclei. But another explanation is that each electron is in itself a magnetic field, though it is only when they behave in a unified manner that the field exerts

---

9 Selections from the Writings of 'Abdu'l-Bahá, (Haifa: Baha'i World Centre, Distributed in the U.S.A, 1978).

an influence beyond itself. [10] This not only tied in to my ongoing contemplation of quantum mechanics and the unity of science and religion, it brought to light that the Bahá'í writings were addressing such topics.

For these and many other reasons, I continued to be fascinated by what I was learning from the Bahá'ís.

True disciples of Christ, I had previously concluded, would allow themselves to be led wherever God wanted them to go, to accomplish whatever it was that He wanted them to accomplish. And this could be very different for each individual. People who have the Sign of Christ would not judge other individuals. They would not typically be found within groups that do. *The Hardness of the Heart* carefully explains how the parable of the sheep and the goats illustrates this. The sheep and the goats are separated by whether or not they judged someone else as being worthy or unworthy of their love and care. And the sheep were not concerned about whether someone else exemplified Christ in their life or not; they treated others with the respect they would if that person were Christ, whoever that person was. [11]

Again, the Bahá'ís seemed to pass this test as well. I was increasingly hyper-aware that I had been asking God for years to help me find Christ's disciples. Could the Bahá'ís be counted among them?

The shocking hypothesis that a faith that doesn't even call itself Christian might fulfill the Sign of the Christian covenant was made more plausible in that the Bahá'í Faith did explicitly embrace Christ. Of course, that isn't good enough for orthodox Christianity, with its creeds and doctrines and litmus tests. But then I had already been weaving my way carefully through what the Bible actually says to avoid the traps set by orthodoxy for those who trust the text more than tradition.

Without wishing to force the issue or a conclusion on it, I spent considerable time in the first two volumes of this trilogy on exhibit A in the case against orthodoxy—namely, that Christ gave three days and three nights in the grave as proof of who He was. This is rejected by the Friday night crucifixion, Sunday morning resurrection creed that, historically, all orthodox Christians had to accept. If those who, throughout history, have claimed Christ most fervently have creeds that reject this Sign, where do we go with this?

A shorthand version of how to address this thorny problem, without driving offense and disunity, would be to say that Bahá'ís accept that Christ is everything He claimed to be, while not judging others on what they did or didn't believe, specifically and explicitly, about Christ. That was why I, as a Christian,

---

10 Brian Skinner, "Where Does Magnetism Come From?," *Gravity and Levity* (blog), April 19, 2015, https://gravityandlevity.wordpress.com/2015/04/19/where-does-magnetism-come-from/.
11 See Matthew 25:31-44.

was able to continue exploring the Bahá'í faith, even though there were open questions.

One of the big issues for me at that time was that religions, even if they originate with God, become corrupt over time. The one problem I still saw in the Bahá'í emphasis on love and unity was in how it tended to downplay the negative impact of this corruption of religion. This had always been a concern of mine due to the history of the Christian tradition and was a growing concern for everyone, given the growing impact of radical Islam on the world scene.

This loving acceptance was important for human relationships, but how can unity exist between corrupt systems that are diametrically opposed to each other? Bob Dylan sang of Christianity in "Tight Connection to My Heart" that he "never could learn to drink that blood and call it wine." His simple, elegant, and powerful use of these symbols in this manner highlighted the hypocrisy of how what we profess is so often in opposition to what we do. Reviewing his lyrics in the light of how religion has further evolved (or devolved) since he penned those lines, we see how far off base large segments of Islam have become, with twisted beliefs about jihad and martyrdom that create suicidal terrorists. They take the analogy of wolves in sheep's clothing to a new extreme.

POWER TO THE PEOPLE

With regard to the Christian faith, Bahá'ís, along with most others, can point positively to its influence on the growth of Western civilization, without recognizing that it too took on an extremely corrupt form very early on and that as a religion it committed great evils. In the case of Islam, Bahá'ís acknowledge that Islam was hijacked at the death of its founder, while, from my perspective, they are very hesitant to acknowledge the horror it has become in much of the world.

At the same time, as stated above, the perspective of the Bahá'ís allowed them to graciously fulfill the sign of love. I had great respect, generally, for how they handled such issues, while I grappled with each specific item. It was important to me to identify and locate bridges between my perspective and theirs, so that I could understand the wisdom at the source of views that were often at a polar opposite from mine.

Much to my delight, my new Bahá'í friends seemed to enjoy studying these topics almost as much as I did. For me, it was enlightening to make connections to what I already knew, as I explored what they believed. The stunning realization which I frequently made was that the distance between our viewpoints was more often than not the exact distance that had always, and quite uncomfortably, separated my head and my heart. Views which seemed, on the surface, to be as different as night and day were in fact reconciled by bending the line into a circle and bringing the ends together. The feelings of peace and joy that resulted from each mini-epiphany kept me digging and searching for more.

My primary focus was still my relationship with Angela, who seemed at least as smitten with the Bahá'í Faith as she was with me. But I was equally motivated to make and share connections which were not apparent to the Bahá'ís. With regard to the Mosaic covenant, for example, Bahá'ís accepted it as a religion of God but too often seemed to dismiss or diminish it as being so ancient in the context of "progressive revelation" as to have little importance in today's world. This did little to improve on Christianity's view of Judaism as obsolete.

While I felt very welcome and accepted by the Bahá'ís, too many of them dismissed much of the Bible as myth. Many others emphasized its symbolic value or highlighted vague moral principles. This was in sharp contrast to my view, which was that these ancient texts contained chapter after chapter of detailed prophetic information, the specific detail of which couldn't possibly be more relevant today. If there were any truth to what Bahá'ís believed about the Báb and Bahá'u'lláh, then I would expect their writings to corroborate my position, not theirs.

Challenging conventional wisdom had always motivated me. Further study of the Bahá'í writings did indeed lead me to some very different perspectives than those commonly held by my new friends. One very pointed example of this was what I eventually learned the Bahá'í writings say about the Beast's power in Revelation.

Bahá'u'lláh's son, 'Abdu'l-Bahá, wrote a large number of books and letters. In one compilation called *Some Answered Questions*, he identifies the Beast as "the Umayyads."[12] This is the first Islamic dynasty, the Caliphate, which has given rise to what the world knows of as Islam today, including often brutal and repressive regimes that bring to mind the worst of religious oppression throughout the ages, and which has most recently metastasized into ISIS. 'Abdu'l-Bahá thus, in my view, seems to state that the religion Muhammed brought was kidnapped and perverted by his successors, and also reveals that what arose in its stead, what the world knows as Islam is, in fact, the Beast of Revelation.

---

12 "The beast that ascendeth out of the bottomless pit shall war against them, and shall overcome them, and kill them": this beast means the Umayyads who attacked them from the pit of error, and who rose against the religion of Muḥammad and against the reality of 'Alí—in other words, the love of God." (From Bahá'í Reference Library, "11: Commentary on the Eleventh Chapter of the Revelation of St. John," page 51, accessed June 29, 2018, http://reference.bahai.org/en/t/ab/SAQ/saq-11.html.)

This view is unknown or misunderstood by a shocking number of Bahá'ís. As time goes on and global Islamists wreak ever more havoc and infiltrate more and more countries to a higher degree, this view is becoming more mainstream, even as it also becomes more polarizing.

Exposure to Bahá'í beliefs had encouraged the use of a wide aperture, allowing me to view all religion as pieces of one common pot, shattered and spread across the planet at the Tower of Babel. My lifelong study into the specifics of and the relationship between two of these pieces, Judaism and Christianity, was a valuable asset in a Bahá'í context. Most Bahá'ís appreciated my ability to make a contribution to a group effort to put the puzzle together. And the group I was in contained people educated in the specifics of other religions, which meant a number of pieces were accurately falling into place.

Perhaps the most important piece of this puzzle was the understanding that the Sabbath Sign, the bridge that was supposed to lead Israel to Christ was simultaneously a bridge to understanding the many prophecies related to Israel. Their adherence to the Sign of their covenant was a key by which God ensured that Judaism would survive the advent of Christianity to play a dominant positive role in end-time events.

In other words, it became clear that the Sign of the Sabbath was something intended to be carried forward by the people to whom it was actually given.

That the nation of Israel exists today suddenly became an almost blinding source of prophetic light.

Dress Me Up as a Robber

Three things cannot be long hidden: the sun, the moon, and the truth.

—BUDDHA

In the WCG we had tried to understand prophecy by identifying the lost ten tribes of Israel. We believed that the ten tribes that had comprised the Northern Kingdom of ancient Israel had lost their identity because they had not kept the Sign of the covenant, the Sabbath day. Now it became blindingly clear that the identity of these Lost Tribes was not the key at all. Why guess at the identity of that which was lost and hidden, when God had given a Sign, the Sabbath, for the purpose of establishing identity? In fact, the Sign was to be prominent, because many passages explained that keeping His commandments would result in Israel being exalted among the nations.

The Sabbath was quite obviously intended to identify and keep Israel in clear view. Today's Jews are largely the descendants of the two-and-a-half tribes that formed the Southern Kingdom, called Judah, along with outcasts from Israel who had held fast to the original teachings (i.e., the Sign).[1] They were not lost. They were clearly visible. And they were active on the world scene. How had we gotten that backwards?

YOU WON'T SEE ME

The descendants of the kingdom of Judah in modern times have assumed the identity of all Israel. Israel is the key to understanding prophecy. So why

1 See *Encyclopaedia Britannica*, s.v. "Ten Lost Tribes of Israel," last updated November 13, 2013, https://www.britannica.com/topic/Ten-Lost-Tribes-of-Israel. See also "Are Today's Jews Genetically Descended from the Biblical Israelites?," One for Israel, accessed May 11, 2018, https://www.oneforisrael.org/bible-based-teaching-from-israel/todays-jews-genetically-descended-khazars/.

isn't it more obvious to everyone that the modern nation of Israel is the key that unlocks prophetic understanding?

Those in the WCG and COG movement actually saw this, but the blindness that kept us from realizing it and its importance seemed to be our emphasis on our own righteousness. Our inflated view of our own attempts to keep the Sabbath and Holy Days led us to exalt ourselves and put others down. Our bias was to view ourselves as being at the forefront of prophetic fulfillment. We were doing the Work of God, which blinded us to what God was actually doing.

There is a similarity to this across many other Christian denominations. They are influenced directly or indirectly by replacement theology. Replacement theology is the idea, based on a misinterpretation of the writings of Paul, that Christians have replaced Israel and the Jews in the plan of God. Paul writes, for example, that we have been "grafted in" to the tree and are participants in the promises made to Israel. Those statements seem, on the surface, to lean in a replacement direction, but a simple read of the entire chapter of Romans 11, in which this statement is contained, reveals that the branches are not the root and warns the partakers against becoming usurpers. Most importantly, the current facts on the ground prove replacement theology wrong. The existence of a state of Israel, populated by Jews, which has arrived according to the prophetic timeline, is convincing evidence that replacement theology is not true.

Many nations, peoples, and religions today deny, to varying degrees, the reality of the prophetic miracle that is the nation of Israel. I had never been among them but never before had this miracle seized my full attention. Now it did.

It was time for me to take a fresh look at the book of Isaiah, a monumental and challenging book, which, among other things, underscores the importance of Israel's prophetic role in God's long-term plan for humankind. The following section from chapter 56 highlights the Sabbath as a critical sign that enables the fulfillment of promises made to Israel:

Thus says the Lord: "Keep justice, and do righteousness, for My salvation is about to come, and My righteousness to be revealed. Blessed is the man who does this, and the son of man who lays hold on it; who keeps from defiling the Sabbath, and keeps his hand from doing any evil." Do not let the son of the foreigner who has joined himself to the Lord speak, saying, "The Lord has utterly separated me from His people"; nor let the eunuch say, "Here I am, a dry tree." For thus says the Lord: "To the eunuchs who keep My Sabbaths, and choose what pleases Me, and hold fast My covenant, even to them I will give in My house and within My walls a place and a name better than that of sons and daughters; I will give them an everlasting name that shall not be cut off. Also the sons of the foreigner who join themselves to the Lord, to serve Him, and to love the name of the Lord, to be His servants—everyone who keeps from defiling the Sabbath, and holds fast My covenant—even them I will bring to My holy mountain, and make them joyful in My house of prayer. Their burnt offerings and their sacrifices will be accepted on My altar; for My house shall be called a house of prayer for all nations." The Lord God, who gathers the outcasts of Israel, says, "Yet I will gather to him others besides those who are gathered to him."[2]

Those who keep Jewish law, typified by the Sabbath—the Sign of the Mosaic covenant—become part of Israel. Those who don't—and who substitute Sunday for Saturday, among other things, do not. The people who actually hold fast to this Sign are today known as Jews. Even those of the Jewish community who do not keep the Sign are thus identified as the People of the Sign.

They held fast to their covenant, even in the face of the most horrific persecutions ever perpetrated against any people. The magnitude of this simple truth dawned on me slowly over time, leading me ultimately to reflect deeply on the serious admonitions not to claim titles that do not belong to us.[3]

In the first two volumes of this trilogy, I generally avoided the muddy and treacherous waters of biblical prophecy. To move forward from here, we've got to move on from dipping our toes into it and proceed now to get our feet thoroughly wet. The "Great Disappointment" is as good a place to start as any.

ANY TIME AT ALL

The Great Disappointment was preceded by a Protestant movement known as the first Great Awakening. It began sweeping Protestant Europe and British America in 1730 and 1740, energizing those who were already members of the Protestant churches. A second Great Awakening began around 1790, primarily in the United States, which brought many unchurched people into mainly Baptist and Methodist congregations, places where preachers led the movement. This in turn led to movements to reform society before the anticipated second coming of Jesus Christ. One prominent man rode this wave of religious zeal into prophetic history:

---

2 Isaiah 56:1-8 NKJV.
3 Revelation 2:9: "I know thy works, and tribulation, and poverty, (but thou art rich) and I know the blasphemy of them which say they are Jews, and are not, but are the synagogue of Satan." Revelation 3:9: "Behold, I will make them of the synagogue of Satan, which say they are Jews, and are not, but do lie; behold, I will make them to come and worship before thy feet, and to know that I have loved thee."

Between 1831 and 1844, on the basis of his study of the Bible, and particularly the prophecy of Daniel 8:14—"Unto two thousand and three hundred days; then shall the sanctuary be cleansed"—William Miller, a Baptist preacher, predicted and preached the imminent return of Jesus Christ to the earth. ... Using an interpretive principle known as the day-year principle, Miller, along with others, interpreted a prophetic "day" to read not as a 24-hour period, but rather as a calendar year. Miller became convinced that the 2,300-day period started in 457 B.C. with the decree to rebuild Jerusalem by Artaxerxes I of Persia. Simple calculation revealed that this period would end—and hence Christ would return—in 1843. [4]

Herbert W. Armstrong, who founded the WCG, owed a huge debt to William Miller, who, rather than adopt a sensationalist approach, actually resisted pressure from supporters to announce an exact date for the second coming.[5] Miller did, however, "narrow the time period to sometime in the Jewish year 5604, stating: 'My principles in brief, are, that Jesus Christ will come again to this earth, cleanse, purify, and take possession of the same, with all the saints, sometime between March 21, 1843 and March 21, 1844.'"[6]

Armstrong retained Miller's essential framework, including the day for a year principle but perhaps learning from the Great Disappointment, or perhaps, unlike Miller, not having any clear date to use, he took a different approach. Beginning in the 1930s he had an amazing fifty-year run of predictions that Christ would return "in the next 5, 10 to 15 years." During this time, Armstrong and his followers kept the zeal of the WCG alive by claiming to be the "One True Church" and channeled the excitement of a prediction of Christ's imminent return, and this exclusivity claim, into the creation of a global media presence to warn the world.

Having been admittedly somewhat gullible with regard to such predictions, one of my fears about the Bahá'í Faith turned out to be true. The founder, an Iranian nobleman named Bahá'u'lláh, had claimed to be the fulfillment of prophecies related to the return of Christ. It was not hard for me to reject this claim to my satisfaction, not only because the world around us didn't reflect the arrival of the Kingdom of God on earth but also because Christ had specifically warned against what to me seemed to be this exact kind of

---

4 Martin, "Matthew 24:35-37 Time of the Second Coming," Bible Guide for the New Age (blog), January 01, 1970, accessed June 29, 2018, http://bibleguidefornewage.blogspot.com/2014/11/matthew-2435-37-time-of-second-coming.html.

5 *Encyclopaedia Britannica Online*, s.v. "William Miller," accessed June 29, 2018, https://www.britannica.com/biography/William-Miller.

6 *https://www.amazon.com/Sketches-Christian-gathered-Sylvester-sources/dp/1425545807.*

claim.[7] Rejecting this out of hand, even if I kept this opinion to myself, created a clear boundary that actually made it easier to associate freely with the Bahá'ís. This ease was also because they weren't trying to convince me of anything, given that they firmly and unequivocally believed in the principle of the independent investigation of truth.

But as I've mentioned before, I was driven to investigate further by what I learned about that John the Baptist–like figure called the Báb, whose purpose, according to Bahá'ís, was to announce the arrival of Bahá'u'lláh. The Báb is considered to be a full "Manifestation of God" by Bahá'ís, putting him on an equal station with Moses, Mohammed, Christ, and others. And yet the role of the Báb was to establish a fast-growing independent religion, just like all his predecessors, but unlike them in duration. While asserting a claim to be the "Promised One"—the Qá'im, or Mahdi, of Shia Islam—the Báb's focus was on an imminent successor. His religion was to last but a very short while, with an intense John the Baptist–like focus on someone most frequently called "Him whom God will make manifest." Bábís were to turn to this new Manifestation, promised in the books of all religions, who would establish the Kingdom of God on earth.[8] This was to take place in two steps, nine and nineteen years after the Báb's declaration.

And you'll recall that the Báb declared in 1844.

BABY IT'S YOU

The Báb was martyred in Shiraz in 1850, and Bahá'u'lláh was imprisoned shortly thereafter, in a notoriously dark and fetid underground dungeon in Tehran called the Síyáh-Chál (Black Pit). There, nine years after the Báb's declaration, Bahá'u'lláh had several mystical visions signifying to him that he was "Him whom God will make manifest." Bahá'u'lláh eventually declared this openly in 1863—19 years after the Báb's declaration.

These references to the number nineteen further piqued my interest, given the WCG emphasis, in prophetic interpretation, on nineteen-year time cycles. And when I learned that the Báb instituted a calendar, adopted by the Bahá'ís, with nineteen days and nineteen months, I was quite

---

7 Matthew 24:23-28: "Then if any man shall say unto you, Lo, here is Christ, or there; believe it not. For there shall arise false Christs, and false prophets, and shall shew great signs and wonders; insomuch that, if it were possible, they shall deceive the very elect. Behold, I have told you before. Wherefore if they shall say unto you, Behold, he is in the desert; go not forth: behold, he is in the secret chambers; believe it not. For as the lightning cometh out of the east, and shineth even unto the west; so shall also the coming of the Son of man be. For wheresoever the carcase is, there will the eagles be gathered together."
8 J. E. Esslemont, Bahá'u'lláh and the New Era, (US Bahá'í Publishing Trust, 1980 edition).

surprised that many Bahá'ís hadn't made a connection to the nineteen-year Metonic cycle.[9]

This cycle is a complicated calculation of one complete revolution of the divine clock called the solar system, based on the moon's position in the sky. The nineteen-year connection between the Báb and Bahá'u'lláh encouraged my suspicion that major prophetic significance was woven into the fabric of space-time at that critical juncture.

Despite the WCG's use of prophetic interpretation in a broad, general way, we had never looked seriously at the 1844 date. Now, with what the Bahá'ís had to say about it, it was like a big red *X* on a pirate's map, marking a spot at which I was supposed to dig deeper.

When I asked Bahá'ís about this date, they were quick to point out two major coincidences. The declaration of the Báb on May 23, 1844, coincided exactly with the birth of Bahá'u'lláh's son, 'Abdu'l-Bahá. He was known as "the Master" and had succeeded Bahá'u'lláh as the "Center of the Covenant." This coincidence was intriguing enough, but the second coincidence had a more immediately powerful impact on me.

The very first telegraph message, they explained, was sent the next day, on May 24, signifying for Bahá'ís that word of these events traveled like lightning from east to west. This, they believed, fulfilled part of the passage I cited earlier, from Matthew 24, a cornerstone in my rejection of Bahá'u'lláh's claims. And now, just over one hundred years after his death, millions of people had traveled to Haifa, on pilgrimage, corresponding to the subsequent verse about the eagles gathering.[10]

Because I privately, without serious consideration, rejected Bahá'u'lláh's claims, I skeptically looked into this telegraph message. Sure enough, inventor Samuel F. B. Morse sent the first telegraphic message over an experimental line from Washington DC to Baltimore, on May 24, 1844, the day after the declaration by the Gate of God. And there did seem to be an eerie connection to Matthew's "as the lightning cometh out of the east, and shineth even unto the west."

The direction the message traveled was not only east to west, but the method used was electricity, which is about as close to the way lightning travels as you can get. President Abraham Lincoln even referred to messages sent by telegraph as "lightning messages," a point validated by the US Office of the State–Department of the Historian, which states, "The most significant characteristic

---

9 Encyclopaedia Britannica Online, s.v. "Metonic cycle," accessed June 29, 2018, https://www.britannica.com/science/Metonic-cycle.

10 Matthew 24:27-28: "For as the lightning cometh out of the east, and shineth even unto the west; so shall also the coming of the Son of man be. For wheresoever the carcase is, there will the eagles be gathered together."

of the telegraph was its speed. Telegrams traveled like lightning across continents and oceans." [11]

This was not something I could just dismiss out of hand simply because it seemed so fantastic, which brings us back to William Miller.

A May 2011 *Time* magazine article listed the "Top 10 End-of-the-World Prophecies."[12] William Miller got top billing, because, as the article states:

> as many as 100,000 "Millerites" sold their belongings between 1840 and 1844 and took to the mountains to wait for the end. When that end didn't come, some of Miller's followers changed the date to Oct. 22.

When Oct. 23 rolled around, the disappointment of those who had placed that particular bet came up with a rather convoluted explanation, which became a cornerstone teaching within the Seventh-day Adventist movement, which grew out of Millerism after his death. Miller himself never gave up hope, and died December 20, 1849, faithfully waiting for Christ's coming, based on his unshaken belief that his calculations were essentially correct.[13]

Even in my WCG days, when we as a movement tended to look down on those silly people who had gathered in 1844, I always felt that that William Miller had gotten a bum rap. There was legitimacy to the claim that Daniel and other prophecies pointed to 1844, and nobody had ever given me a clear answer on how it could be interpreted to be a date other than 1844. At the same time, despite the apparently legitimate math pointing to 1844, I had never before heard a credible claim that anything important had happened in 1844. Now I was confronted with an entire group that was putting forward the claim that that something had. And the verse I had used to brush away those claims now seemed, instead, to support them.

And that wasn't all.

---

11 "U.S. Diplomacy and the Telegraph, 1866," Office of the Historian, US State Department, accessed May 11, 2018, https://history.state.gov/milestones/1866-1898/telegraph.

12 Kayla Webley, "Top 10 End-of-the-World Prophecies," Time, Friday May 20, 2011, http://content.time.com/time/specials/packages/article/0,28804,2072678_2072683,00.html.

13 Note that Time Magazine is less generous than other sources in its assessment of whether Miller set dates or not. As an aside, at a time when the term "fake news" is tossed around, careful attention to facts and details is important, as bias, slant, and spin are important factors in any attempt to get to the truth of the matter. It is the author's position that it is extremely rare that any information is presented without bias. On the subject of Herbert Armstrong, for example, many today refer to him as a false prophet, because many of his predictions did not come to pass. On the other hand, he repeatedly emphasized that he did not consider himself to be a prophet. The decision to take a position on that, one way or another is up to the individual. However, care should be taken before adopting a position on whatever topic is being presented, and a fair-minded person will perhaps be less emphatic, less dogmatic, and more detached than someone with more attachment to the topic. For those who wish to learn more about William Miller, the original Adventist movement, and a key precursor to the Bahá'í Faith, I recommend Carolyn Sparey Fox, The Half of It Was Never Told (Oxford: George Ronald, 2015).

The text of the first telegraph message appeared to be almost as significant as the connection to the prophecy about lightning. The message Samuel F. B. Morse sent on May 24, 1844, was "What hath God wrought?" Annie Ellsworth, the young daughter of a friend, had suggested the sentence to Morse.

When I looked up this obscure Bible verse, I found it in Numbers 23:23. I was quite familiar with the story from which this verse was taken, and it suggested a lot more going on underneath the surface. In fact, it sent shivers up and down my spine.

ONE AFTER 909

The full text of Numbers 23:23 is this: "Surely there is no enchantment against Jacob, neither is there any divination against Israel: according to this time it shall be said of Jacob and of Israel, What hath God wrought!"

William Miller's 2,300-year calculation that led to 1844 began in 457 BC, with the decree to rebuild Jerusalem by Artaxerxes I of Persia. That strange name "Babel" features heavily in this intriguing puzzle piece.

Eschatology, according to Merriam-Webster, is "a branch of theology concerned with the final events in the history of the world or of humankind." Biblical eschatology weaves the return of Christ and the return of Israel to the Holy Land into an intricate tapestry. The images of this tapestry are beautiful and inspiring to those who look to God for deliverance.

At the same time, it is difficult to separate the threads that form the spiritual and the literal. This challenge tripped up the Pharisees and other religious leaders of Jesus's day, for example, who were looking for a physical Messiah who would reestablish Israel's greatness. While it would likely bore most readers if I carefully and meticulously traced all the threads that form this tapestry, one prominent thread that must be considered is the story of Zerubbabel:

> **Zerubbabel:** the head of the tribe of Judah at the time of the return from the Babylonish captivity in the first year of Cyrus. The history of Zerabbabel [sic] in the Scriptures is as follows: In the first year of Cyrus he was living at Babylon, and was the recognized prince of Judah in the captivity, —what in later times was called "the prince of the captivity," or "the prince." On the issuing of Cyrus' decree he immediately availed himself of it, and placed himself at the head of those of his countrymen "whose spirit God had raised to go up to build the house of the Lord which is in Jerusalem."[14]

---

14 *Smith's Bible Dictionary*, s.v. "Zerubbabel" accessed May 11, 2018, https://www.christianity.com/bible/dictionary.php?dict=sbd&id=4579.

King Darius I of Persia appointed Zerubbabel governor of the province of Judah, and it is assumed that widespread revolts at the beginning of the reign of Darius I in 522 BC preoccupied him to such a degree that Zerubbabel felt he could initiate the rebuilding of the temple without repercussions. Zerubbabel was closely associated with the high priest who returned with him, Joshua son of Jozadak, but he was a civil not a religious leader. There are subtly variant definitions of exactly what his name means—the Greek version seems to be "born at Babel," and the Hebrew "sown in Babylon."[15]

My perspective on Zerubbabel was colored by the general view of the history of Israel as one of disobedience and failure, resulting in a corruption and a lack of purity that kept them from ever fulfilling God's will for them as a people. For me, the name of the leader of this mini-revival of the fortunes of Israel symbolized compromise with enemies both politically and religiously. These new connections, and the understanding that God constantly worked with imperfect human beings and situations to accomplish His plan, forced a reevaluation of this view.

Zerubbabel now appeared to be an important and clear prophetic connection between the earliest biblical records of human society right through to the establishment of the Kingdom of God. His name hearkened back to the prophetic significance of Babel while his activities foreshadowed the future. He seemed to be a forerunner to the role Israel was playing—as a civil nation in opposition to, even though established under, the reign of Babylon the Great. This seemed an astounding parallel to modern Israel.[16] The return of the Jews to the Holy Land was almost certainly an important key to unlock the answers to the questions that seemed more important than ever.

Aside from the 2,300 years focused on by Miller, there are other important prophetic timelines, which parallel this. There is the "seven times punishment" from Leviticus, 2,520 years—also known as the longest prophecy—which is generally calculated anywhere from the Battle of Carchemish in 605 BC through successive deportations and the imprisonment of King Jehoiachin in

---

15 *Strong's Hebrew Lexicon (KJV)*, s.v. "H2216, Zĕrubbabel," accessed May 11, 2018, https://www.blueletterbible.org/lang/lexicon/lexicon.cfm?Strongs=H2216&t=KJV. See also "Zerubbabel Meaning," Abarim Publications, accessed May 11, 2018, http://www.abarimpublications.com/Meaning/Zerubbabel.html#.WsGaUS7wbIU.

16 One of the eerie parallels, as we will see shortly, is what James M. Gray writes: "We already have seen that the Babylonian captivity did not bring the Jews to national repentance, and so lead to national restoration. As the reading of Ezra will disclose, when Cyrus, king of Persia, gave permission to the captives to return to Jerusalem and rebuild the Temple, scarcely 50,000 availed themselves of the privilege, a considerable portion of whom were priests and Levites of the humbler and poorer class." James M. Gray, quoted in J. Vernon McGee, "Notes for Ezra," accessed May 11, 2018, https://www.blueletterbible.org/Comm/mcgee_j_vernon/notes-outlines/ezra/ezra-notes.cfm?a=406002.

Babylon in 562.[17] This lengthy period of punishment for disobedience began with their conquest. This means the end of Israel's punishment might have come anywhere from 1915 to as late as 1958. And there are other interpretations which seek to tie this exactly to the modern history of Israel.[17]

The Jews are arguably the most consistently persecuted people across human history. They were oppressed, persecuted, and almost annihilated multiple times. Even the glorious Magna Carta Libertatum, which is Medieval Latin for "the Great Charter of the Liberties," enshrined eight anti-Semitic clauses.[18]

The anti-Semitism of that time resulted in King Edward I, in 1290, expelling the 2,500 Jews who lived in England. The majority left for France, which was a safe haven for a while. In recent history, systematic oppression and ethnic cleansing began with pogroms lasting almost one hundred years in the Russian empire, from 1821 to the early 1900s, followed, of course, by Hitler's Holocaust, which was actually embraced by Hungary's Admiral Horthy and others in Europe and elsewhere.[19]

The devastated remnants of this people assembled from all over the world in the desert wasteland that was the Holy Land in the early to mid-1900s. Somehow, against all odds, they were able to cobble together a nation in what was to become a geopolitical hotbed like no other. And they survived repeated assaults by groups of nations, each much larger and more powerful.

I was increasingly becoming aware of what is already considered a miracle by many—the establishment and survival of the Jewish state. Despite all this, they managed not only to establish themselves in the Holy Land as a nation but to survive and thrive, against all odds and against all opposition. And this miracle had begun with the Edict of Toleration, issued by the Ottoman Empire in 1844.

TILL THERE WAS YOU

There is yet another important prophetic timeline, which begins later than the period of Israel's punishment and ends a bit earlier. I'm referring to the "times of the Gentiles."

---

17 Ezekiel 2520 Prophecy," Servant of Messiah Ministries, accessed July 2, 2018, http://servantofmessiah.org/times-and-seasons/prophetic-studies/ezekiel-2520-israel-1948/.

18 Rachel X. Landes, "8 Jewish Things About the Magna Carta on Its 800th Anniversary," The Schmooze (blog), June 15, 2015, https://forward.com/schmooze/310072/8-jewish-facts-about-the-magna-carta-on-its-800th-anniversary/.

19 Aleksandar Veljic, Genocide Revealed (City: Something or Other Publishing, 2015), https://www.amazon.com/Genocide-Revealed-Massacre-Hungarian-Occupation/dp/0984693815. One title that was being considered for the volume was "Hitler's Mentor," because the book explains that Horthy was admired by Hitler and, being considerably older, was anti-Semitic prior to Hitler.

Jesus introduces the term "times of the Gentiles" in Luke 21:24, in the context of the ongoing punishments that began with the "seven times punishments": "And they shall fall by the edge of the sword, and shall be led away captive into all nations: and Jerusalem shall be trodden down of the Gentiles, until the times of the Gentiles be fulfilled." We learn in the book of Revelation that the duration of the times of the Gentiles is forty-two months.[20] During these months, Jerusalem is to be under foreign occupation.

Numerous attempts have been made to use various starting points to calculate the end of the times of the Gentiles. A standard reference for many twentieth century religious groups, especially those with more of a fundamentalist perspective, *The Companion Bible*, also known as the Bullinger Bible, used the same "day-for-a-year" method to calculate the forty-two months, making them 1,260 prophetic years. While Bullinger adopted the siege of Jerusalem by the Rashidun caliphate in AD 636 as the starting point, an alternate view, related to Islam, connected this date to Islamic prophecies about the "Twelfth Imam."

The Shia branch of Islam followed a series of twelve imams, whose authority they traced back to Muhammad. The last of these disappeared in the Islamic year 260 AH. According to a reference in the Qur'an, authority was to be reestablished after one thousand years.[21] For this reason, there was widespread anticipation among Shiites that the Twelfth Imam would return in Islamic year 1260 AH. This is also the year 1844 in the Christian calendar.[22]

The plot was thickening considerably, but it would be a while before I would connect all the dots. One of these was very specifically related to the return of the Jews to the Holy Land, beginning in 1844. I learned about the Edict of Toleration issued by the Ottoman Empire on March 21, 1844, which was seen by the Bahá'í Faith as beginning the process of allowing Jews to settle in the Holy Land.[23]

It is astounding that the Jews have visibly returned to the Holy Land, and Jerusalem is their capital. But this played out over 150 years, and rather than focus on the astounding prophetic nature of this amazing fact, even many of those who do care about it, as we've shown, have their own reasons for denying the obvious.

---

20 Revelation 11:2 and 13:5.
21 Marzieh Gail, Dawn over Mount Hira (Oxford: George Ronald, 1976), 58.
22 *Wikipedia*, s.v. "Convergence of 1260-Day Prophecy and the 2300-Day Prophecy," in "Day-Year Principle," last updated March 18, 2018, http://en.wikipedia.org/wiki/Day-year_principle#Convergence_of_1260-Day_Prophecy_and_the_2300-Day_Prophecy.
23 Michael Sours, "The 1844 Ottoman 'Edict of Toleration' in Bahá'í Secondary Literature," *Journal of Baha'i Studies* 8, no. 3 (1998): 53–80.

Most who are only marginally interested are distracted by the smoke screen of contention created by the deniers. It is obvious, however, when one blows away the smoke, that those to whom the Sign was actually given and who held fast to it through thousands of years of persecution are clearly the ones prophesied to return and be assembled in the Holy Land. They would represent what Isaiah 11 calls the "ensign for the nations:"

> And it shall come to pass in that day, that the Lord shall set his hand again the second time to recover the remnant of his people, which shall be left, from Assyria, and from Egypt, and from Pathros, and from Cush, and from Elam, and from Shinar, and from Hamath, and from the islands of the sea. And he shall set up an ensign for the nations, and shall assemble the outcasts of Israel, and gather together the dispersed of Judah from the four corners of the earth. The envy also of Ephraim shall depart, and the adversaries of Judah shall be cut off: Ephraim shall not envy Judah, and Judah shall not vex Ephraim.[24]

It is significant that Judah, not Israel, is referenced here. Israel, the Northern Kingdom, had completely abandoned the Sign, while the Southern Kingdom of Judah had held on to it. The Northern Kingdom was lost. Without the Sign, they could not and would not be gathered. There is no need to believe, as we did in the WCG, that large masses of people from the lost ten tribes would return. The true People of the Sign, gathered and forming a state called Israel, were a quite obvious manifestation of the prophesied "ensign for the nations." Yet questions remained, which took me several years to answer to my satisfaction.

For starters, if the Bahá'í claims were true, why did almost nobody know about the Gate of God's declaration in 1844? Even within Iran, with a large population that fervently expected the appearance of the Twelfth Imam, after the initial surge of conversions to the Bábí faith, ruthless persecution suppressed information related to the Báb's claim, limiting the possibility that all eyes would be opened to the Báb's appearance. And yet all eyes were supposed to see this when it happened.

The Bahá'í answer to this was that Christ was to return not on but in the clouds, like a thief at night.

---

24 Isaiah 11:11-13.

SHE CAME IN THROUGH THE BATHROOM WINDOW

My prior understanding and expectation about the return of Christ was that it would be the most astounding event ever experienced by humankind. Though I had never given sermons elaborating on this topic, I had heard a number of them. Some of them had insisted, for example, using the story of Christ's ascension in Acts 1, that He would be visible in the heavens for a full twenty-four hours, as the planet twirled. Such an astounding supernatural event would literally allow every single human eye to see Him and (figuratively) cause every jaw to drop.

But the Bahá'í reading of "in the clouds" stood this on its head. And even aside from the silliness of the spectacle of a supernaturally hovering Christ, it immediately clicked with me that the Bahá'í interpretation of this verse was the right one, as I mentally reviewed the story of Christ's ascent.

The story hinges on the image of the two men in white apparel, standing next to the disciples who are staring at the sky trying to catch a glimpse of the receding Christ. After slowly ascending, He had grown smaller and smaller, until He was gone from their sight, leaving them peering into the sky, straining for some sign of Him. I remembered that one of the men had explained that Christ would return "in like manner," which, upon reflection, indicated a slow reveal rather than a shocking entrance. When I looked up the passage, the story gave even more credence to the Bahá'í interpretation than I had initially realized.

There, in black and white, it said, "While they beheld, he was taken up; and a cloud received him out of their sight."[25] This was further biblical evidence to dispel the idea that everyone would recognize Christ at once for who He was. The Bahá'í view that He would for a time remain hidden in the clouds was more biblically accurate.

While I had to admit that these verses the Bahá'ís cited lent themselves to their position, I wasn't really buying it. The prophecies related to Christ returning with a "rod of iron," both to break the nations in pieces like a clay pot and to subsequently rule them, were far too prominent in my theology for me to accept that He had returned in 1844, only to be roundly ignored. If He had returned, surely the nations wouldn't be allowed to continue going about their selfish, greedy, and often murderous business, as though He had never arrived. For starters, the Iranians would not have been able to suppress the news.

---

25 Acts 1:9.

And yet, on the other hand, I recently read a post in a discussion on biblical prophecy that reminded me its fulfillment is always easily recognized after the fact. And while this is undoubtedly true, it is equally true that it is rarely recognized immediately when it happens. Christ's arrival, some two thousand years ago, was recognized by almost nobody. Anyone who was anybody dismissed Him. It took hundreds of years before He achieved what we would call mainstream acceptance. Could it be that the arrival of widespread recognition at His second coming would be similar? If so, what would bring such recognition about? Does the Bible give us any clues?

We've already discussed the importance of the tribes that weren't lost, that had honored their covenant. Israel was actually the sign that God had given "to the nations." Israel had become a lightning rod since then, attracting the hate of virtually the entire world of Islam and the disdain of most of those who do not believe in God and even a large portion of Christianity. As I complete this section, we have just witnessed US recognition of Jerusalem as the capital of this nation, and the subsequent denouncement at the United Nations. Even down to today, after becoming a powerful, successful nation, anti-Semitism and persecution continues, even at the United Nations.[26] All eyes are indeed on Israel in a way that is truly astounding.

From this perspective, it should be easy to see why, given my familiarity with Israel and prophecy, even in 2006 I could not easily dismiss the Bahá'í claim that something of enormous prophetic significance had indeed happened in 1844, even if the majority of humankind was oblivious. Yet this raised another series of questions.

---

26 David Harris, "Ten Ways Israel Is Treated Differently," *Huffington Post* (blog), June 14, 2016, https://www.huffingtonpost.com/david-harris/ten-ways-israel-is-treate_b_7579568.html.

Free as a Bird

O MY SERVANT! Free thyself from the fetters of this world, and loose thy soul from the prison of self. Seize thy chance, for it will come to thee no more.

BAHÁ'U'LLÁH - *THE HIDDEN WORDS,* PERSIAN NO. 40

If indeed the times of the Gentiles ended in 1844, why did it take more than one hundred years to establish a nation?

Why the Holocaust?

Was there a connection?

BABY'S IN BLACK

Before I provide the answer to the questions I just raised, it's important to soften the blow of the answer. Prophecy not only makes hard truth clear but also palatable, by looking past the horror it so often reveals to the future it proclaims. One analogy used in some prophecies is that of childbirth. The pain is vividly pictured, but the focus is on the baby. While childbirth isn't referenced in what God says to Jews in Isaiah 40:1-8, the passage has a similar feel:

> Comfort ye, comfort ye my people, saith your God. Speak ye comfortably to Jerusalem, and cry unto her, that her warfare is accomplished, that her iniquity is pardoned: for she hath received of the LORD's hand double for all her sins. The voice of him that crieth in the wilderness, Prepare ye the way of the LORD, make straight in the desert a highway for our God. Every valley shall be exalted,

and every mountain and hill shall be made low: and the crooked shall be made straight, and the rough places plain: And the glory of the LORD shall be revealed, and all flesh shall see it together: for the mouth of the LORD hath spoken it.

This glorious vision is interrupted as the voice of "him crying in the wilderness" shifts its tone:

The voice said, Cry. And he said, What shall I cry? All flesh is grass, and all the goodliness thereof is as the flower of the field: The grass withereth, the flower fadeth: because the spirit of the LORD bloweth upon it: surely the people is grass. The grass withereth, the flower fadeth: but the word of our God shall stand for ever.

Dual prophetic timelines seem to have created an approximately one-hundred-year period between 1844, when the Jews were allowed to start returning, and 1948, when the nation of Israel was formed. This was due to the times of the Gentiles ending in 1844, while the "seven times" punishment wouldn't run its course until somewhere between 1917 and 1958.

And this particular framework brought a rather horrific scenario to mind.

There were trickles of Jewish immigration into the Holy Land beginning in 1844 and accelerating into 1881 and again with the "second Aliya"—or "ascent"—from 1904–1914. So twin proclamations drove the fulfillment of prophecy—the Edict of Toleration in 1844 and the Balfour Declaration in 1917. These provided the opportunity to fulfill the destiny of the Mosaic covenant. The Jewish population, however, did not respond as quickly as perhaps God intended. One factor was that the dawn of freedom and materialism provided other options that were more appealing. Between 1907 and 1914 almost 1.5 million Jews went through Ellis Island, while only about 20,000 immigrated to Palestine.[1] Many more were enjoying increasing freedom and opportunity right where they were. Even so, even this trickle led to a Jewish majority in Jerusalem, prior to World War I, a seemingly important milestone of which I was not previously aware.

So the gap between the end of the times of the Gentiles and the end of the times of punishment, covered the period of heel dragging by the remnant of Judah—who (for whatever reasons) did not immediately jump at the chance to participate in the promised end-time fulfillment of prophecies made to their ancestors thousands of years earlier. There is a Passover tradition among the Jews, to raise

---

1 Gur Alroey, "Galveston and Palestine: Immigration and Ideology in the Early Twentieth Century," *American Jewish Archives Journal* 56 (2004): 139.

a glass and toast the prayer "L'Shanah Haba'ah B'Yerushalayim"—"next year in Jerusalem". Sadly, when it began to be possible to actually fulfill this prayer, too many were unwilling or unable to act on this.

The reason for the horrifying finale to the 2,520 years of punishment was, at risk of oversimplifying, that Israel didn't do what God asked. This is not to say that I believe God brought about any of the calamities which have befallen the Jewish people over history. Sadly, it seemed enough to simply remove the divine hand of protection and allow history to take its course.

Those Jews who ignored the early warning signs emanating from Russia at the turn of the twentieth century were caught in the trap of a much more vicious anti-Semitism that swept Europe under the influence and domination of the Nazis. It wasn't until after the full extent of the horrors came to light, and the freedom to travel and emigrate returned, that large numbers of Jews fled to the Holy Land. It was with the temporary and unprecedented support of Jews provided by friendly nations, aghast at what we as a species had done, that the nation of modern Israel was born.

NOBODY TOLD ME

All this seemed to me to be in accordance with the various prophetic time-lines. And it was followed in short order by the success of this tiny, battered people, against the combined forces of more than twenty nations, in the Arab-Israeli War of 1948. The outcome of this and subsequent wars is considered by many to be miraculous. The protective hand of God was clearly not over the Jewish people, globally, prior to and during World War II. Since then, it has been dramatically extended over those who gathered into that geography. And, given the laws of attraction discussed earlier, it's not surprising that the success that resulted under that protection increased the rate of the gathering process.

This amazing fulfillment of prophecies related to the ingathering of Israel was the answer to the question in the text of the first telegraph, from Numbers 23:23: "What hath God Wrought!" This clearly rhetorical question is an exclamation of amazement about that which immediately preceded it within that same verse: "Surely there is no enchantment against Jacob, neither is there any divination against Israel: according to this time it shall be said of Jacob and of Israel, What hath God wrought!" The progress, from that time, in the reestablishment of that tiny state, can only be called, by any standard, miraculous.

During ten years in Germany, I made multiple visits to Dachau, outside Munich, where it is likely that over 200,000 Jewish prisoners were held, and tens of thousands of them died, having their bodies burned in the ovens created to dispose of them.[2] The emotions that surface, even today, upon reflecting on those visits, and others I made to Poland, are overwhelming. I find myself unable to find an appropriate one in describing the enormity of human suffering represented by prophetic history, as experienced by the Jews and the finality of the Holocaust.

Is our inability to acknowledge and comprehend, emotionally, this horror part of the reason so many continue to delegitimize Israel? This question doesn't just refer to Israel's Islamic enemies, who seek to eradicate the Jewish state; I'm referring to those who accept the Bible but fail to recognize that the nation of Israel was established in fulfillment of prophecy.

But there are many reasons for it. The distinction between Israel and Judah is a factor in today's confusion about Israel.[3] We need to address it one last time before we return to the story which led up to the powerful quote "What hath God wrought!" Large sections of the Bible are devoted to this distinction. The sweeping narratives are rich in history and allegory, packing a serious prophetic wallop. Let's review a couple of verses from Isaiah 48, which tie that story to 1844—the passages related to the nation of Israel, the ensign to the nations, which would be delivered through a very painful birth:

> Hear ye this, O house of Jacob, which are called by the name of Israel, and are come forth out of the waters of Judah, which swear by the name of the LORD, and make mention of the God of Israel, but not in truth, nor in righteousness.

A distinction between Israel and Judah (the Jews) is highlighted in the above opening verse of Isaiah 48. Israel is to come forth out of the waters of Judah, even as Judah (Jacob's son) came forth from Israel (the name God gave to Jacob). The Worldwide Church of God missed the point, thinking somehow we needed to identify the lost ten tribes in our modern world and that somehow all of Israel needed to be regathered in the postage stamp–sized piece of real estate known as the Holy Land. Instead, the modern nation of Israel is formed, broadly speaking, of the modern descendants of the southern Kingdom of Judah and a few who left the religiously corrupt

---

2 *Holocaust Encyclopedia*, s.v. "Dachau," United States Holocaust Memorial Museum, accessed May 11, 2018, https://www.ushmm.org/wlc/en/article.php?ModuleId=10005214.
3 Some readers will understandably be puzzled, if not confused, by my distinction between the Jews and Israel. Others, however, especially those with a WCG background, will be intensely interested in this distinction. Here I'm providing an answer without trying to explain why it matters.

Northern Kingdom to join Judah, the people who largely retained the Sign that God gave Israel through Moses.[4]

> I have declared the former things from the beginning; and they went forth out of my mouth, and I shewed them; I did them suddenly, and they came to pass.

The context is this end time, which God has declared from the beginning (i.e., prophecy). Verses 2–9 emphasize the nature of prophecy, with God stating and restating that He declared this ending from the beginning, that they must be punished but that He will not cut them off in the end. This is additional proof that replacement theology is incorrect. And God explains how the outcome, the gathering of the remnant of Israel together under that banner, as a modern state, functions as the "ensign to the nations:"[5]

> Behold, I have refined thee, but not with silver; I have chosen thee in the furnace of affliction.

I believe "the furnace of affliction" is a warning of what was to occur throughout history to the people of both kingdoms (Israel and Judah) with its ultimate end-time fulfillment being Hitler's genocide. Suddenly Judah, the Jews, those who had retained their identity through historic faithfulness to Sign of the Sabbath, were visibly marked by the sickening application of a yellow star.

> For mine own sake, even for mine own sake, will I do it: for how should my name be polluted? and I will not give my glory unto another. Hearken unto me, O Jacob and Israel, my called; I am he; I am the first, I also am the last. Mine

---

4 Isaiah 56 provides further strong support of this view: "For thus says the Lord: 'To the eunuchs who keep My Sabbaths, and choose what pleases Me, and hold fast My covenant, even to them I will give in My house and within My walls a place and a name better than that of sons and daughters; I will give them an everlasting name That shall not be cut off. Also the sons of the foreigner who join themselves to the Lord, to serve Him, and to love the name of the Lord, to be His servants— everyone who keeps from defiling the Sabbath, and holds fast My covenant—even them I will bring to My holy mountain, and make them joyful in My house of prayer. Their burnt offerings and their sacrifices will be accepted on My altar; for My house shall be called a house of prayer for all nations.' The Lord God, who gathers the outcasts of Israel, says, 'Yet I will gather to him others besides those who are gathered to him'" (NKJV).

5 Isaiah 48:2, 4-9: "For they call themselves of the holy city, and stay themselves upon the God of Israel; The Lord of hosts is his name. ... Because I knew that thou art obstinate, and thy neck is an iron sinew, and thy brow brass; I have even from the beginning declared it to thee; before it came to pass I shewed it thee: lest thou shouldest say, Mine idol hath done them, and my graven image, and my molten image, hath commanded them. Thou hast heard, see all this; and will not ye declare it? I have shewed thee new things from this time, even hidden things, and thou didst not know them. They are created now, and not from the beginning; even before the day when thou heardest them not; lest thou shouldest say, Behold, I knew them. Yea, thou heardest not; yea, thou knewest not; yea, from that time that thine ear was not opened: for I knew that thou wouldest deal very treacherously, and wast called a transgressor from the womb. For my name's sake will I defer mine anger, and for my praise will I refrain for thee, that I cut thee not off."

hand also hath laid the foundation of the earth, and my right hand hath spanned the heavens: when I call unto them, they stand up together.

From verse 11 forward we read of God shifting the focus away from the furnaces that led to the birth of the nation, and on to the baby that was to result, again tying in that this was sealed, prophetically, in the framing of every molecule in the universe, the Signs created by space-time.

Later in the chapter, Isaiah ties the future history of Israel back to the deep symbolism of the rock in the desert, out of which the waters, alluded to in the opening verse, were made to supernaturally flow. These waters, supernatural or not, are a lot to swallow. And I'm aware that bringing the Holocaust into this discussion crosses lines of sensitivity; if someone were to assume I am saying things I am emphatically not saying, such as that the Jews somehow deserved or earned this treatment, that would be very offensive indeed. This gives me the opportunity to address one of the biggest philosophical problems I was having with the Bahá'í faith.

HOLD ME TIGHT

The idea that humanity could be brought together by emphasizing the oneness of all religions, the essential unity of religion and science, and a general acceptance of diverse languages and cultures was in opposition to my understanding of why God had done what He did at the Tower of Babel. Hitler, for example was an elected leader. That is but one example of the horror that can be brought about by the wrong kind of unity.

The Tower of Babel story and the record of the Bible, from Genesis to Revelation, are that human beings are biased against God. Apart from God, the world is always standing on the edge of an abyss. Without clear and direct course corrections, misery happens. In the end, Christ would have to return with that "rod of iron" to intervene and stop humanity from committing suicide as a species.

I had now determined, to my satisfaction, that the attitude of nonjudgment adopted so completely and sincerely by the Bahá'ís, as expressed by the acceptance of all religions and cultures, was the right spiritual approach. But to try to build a society on it was another matter entirely. The Bahá'ís had certainly helped me understand that 1844 marked the end of the times of the Gentiles, followed by the full elapse of the 2,520 years of Leviticus one hundred or so years later. This, however, didn't alleviate what to me was a biblical and real-world requirement for Christ, upon His return, to forcefully establish the Kingdom of God and enforce peace upon the warring factions of this planet.

My first impression of the Bahá'ís in America was their quasi-hippie attitude of "love, peace, acceptance, and unity." It felt like they had naively clung to the "anything goes" ethic of the idealistic '60s. This felt like a moral abdication that would ultimately not end well. Humanity, since the Tower of Babel story, had shown itself quite capable of turning a utopian vision into hell on earth. Hitler, Stalin, Chairman Mao, and Pol Pot were but a few examples of this. So, even though I accepted the absolute sincerity of the Bahá'ís I met and the rightness of their spiritual attitude, there was this nagging concern that their movement was inadvertently aligned with those forces that would bring about the ascendancy of the Beast's power. The Bahá'í approach might be just another aspect of abdication of personal and collective responsibility through which humankind fell from sovereignty back into slavery.

Were the Bahá'ís a part of the solution, or were they perhaps part of the problem?

NOT A SECOND TIME

Over time I grew to believe it was the former. This outward attitude among Bahá'ís toward others rested on a solid foundation of spiritual law, which all Bahá'ís were expected to obey. So, while these laws existed and were taught, the Bahá'í community's emphasis was not on obedience to them. They were not deemed binding on non-Bahá'ís anyway. The focus was on absolute love and acceptance, exactly what I had been advocating for years, but from a strong foundation of understanding that obedience is what ultimately leads to happiness.

A perfect example of this balance is the simple Bahá'í marriage vow: "We will all verily abide by the Will of God." It highlights the sanctity of marriage, as a cornerstone of society, and submission to God as the primary focus of Bahá'í life, without any need to further emphasize and define what that is at that moment. Love is in the foreground. Submission to God is explicit and unchallenged. The details of obedience are more private, almost hidden, under a pervasive blanket of love.

But they are there, just under the surface. For example, Angela and I learned early on that Bahá'ís practice strict chastity prior to marriage. It was both reassuring and inconvenient to me at that particular point in my life. It was a clear and unequivocal stance on moral and ethical issues, managed according to principles of love, nonjudgment, purity of heart, and forgiveness. This was exactly what I had advocated in my final years in the ministry, trying to help a very obedience-focused religious group move toward actually fulfilling the Sign of the Christian covenant, love.

There were other very important examples of this. The Bahá'í position on truthfulness is that this is the virtue on which all other virtues depend. And while the laws weren't aggressively enforced, they were clearly articulated, such as in the use of alcohol (prohibited) and drugs (opiates destroy the soul, according to Bahá'ís). These laws were further balanced out by provisions that allowed doctors to override them, through prescriptions to use them, as needed.

Our relationship to material wealth is another key area of opportunity to explore in order to determine whether religious beliefs are sincere. One of the "hidden words" of the Bahá'í Faith is summed this up in a powerful sound bite: "O SON OF BEING! Busy not thyself with this world, for with fire We test the gold, and with gold We test Our servants.[6]"

I was very impressed that no contributions were accepted from non-Bahá'ís, and that this was strictly enforced. Nothing produced by the Bahá'ís, no fund-raisers—whether a car wash, bake sale, or any other event—could be advertised externally to raise money. There was a general fund, which accepted voluntary contributions from Bahá'ís, but no organized Bahá'í group could do anything with the intent of earning or collecting money from outsiders.

Bahá'ís did have a required contribution, a set percentage of their wealth as a one-time donation, after all living expenses were deducted. This was similar to the biblical tithing system, in which Israel received land and was to tithe on the increase from that land, their asset base. The Bahá'í law was implemented on an honor system. You could make this contribution at any time in your life or even at death, and nobody would ever know if you did or didn't contribute according to the proper percentage.

Further, the Bahá'í Faith was administered through representative democratic tiers; locally, nationally, and globally, members had the ability to appeal any decisions up the chain to the Universal House of Justice, which only ever ruled as a majority of five or more out of nine votes. I couldn't imagine a better way to administer this, short of Christ actually presiding. In other words, I could work hand-in-hand with the Bahá'í faith, based on common goals, even if we differed in our understanding about if, how, and when Christ would return and manifest Himself. If anything, they were mitigating the Babylonian system of systems, which worked to subjugate others in favor of those who sought rulership and greater sovereignty over others, even reaching for the heavens

---

6 Bahá'u'lláh - *The Hidden Words*, Arabic no. 55.

to claim a divine authority beyond that which God had granted to each of us, individually.[7]

All of this certainly made what the Bahá'ís were doing very appealing. And if these principles were followed in a global way we would not have a global financial system dominated by what the Bible calls Babylon the Great. This was an important consideration to me, as I've illustrated through my experiences at Deloitte and Countrywide. Now, with GoHuman.com, I was part of a sincere, if perhaps too hopeful and naïve, attempt to launch an alternative. But for me what mattered was whether or not the Bahá'í Faith was from God, not whether or not it appealed to my personal sense of fairness, rightness, sincerity, or any other human standard.

TUG OF WAR

My first view of Israel had been from the deck of the Hellas Express, way back in the summer of 1981, between my freshman and sophomore years at Ambassador College. We approached the harbor at Haifa, and I had eagerly looked for Mount Carmel. After I'd been in Alaska, home of majestic Denali, the tallest mountain on earth, base to peak, Carmel had appeared to be no more than a disappointing hill. The one feature that had stood out was the golden-domed Shrine of the Báb, at the Bahá'í World Center there.

At the time, I asked the late professor Richard Paige, who oversaw student and faculty participation in the City of David Archeological Expedition in the late '70s and early '80s, about the mosque-like structure desecrating Elijah's mountain. Dr. Paige was close friends with Benjamin Mazar of Hebrew University, the first university to feature a degree in Bahá'í studies. Perhaps that is why his answer had been much more neutral than anyone would have expected, given our proclivity, at the time, to view all other religious viewpoints other than our own as satanic deceptions. He told me, "It has some prophetic significance, but we're not sure what it is." I was now so close to an answer to this thirty-year-old riddle that I could almost taste it on my tongue.

The number of puzzle pieces I was considering had expanded enormously. Most of the edge pieces seemed intact, but within it lay scattered fragments of the Tower of Babel, the end of the times of the Gentiles, the religious practice of circumambulation that began at Göbekli Tepe, the role of the Jews (the true People of the Sign), the orbits of the celestial clock—including the lunar, solar,

---

7 For a full explanation of the principles of individual sovereignty and God's original intent that no man or woman should ever rule over another, please see *The Hardness of the Heart*.

and universal calendars—and more. I felt like I had all the pieces I needed, but I still couldn't fit them together.

My personal answer to the connection of all these pieces seemed to hinge on that singular quote that was run through the apparatus that sent it like lightning, from east to west, the day after the Gate of God proclaimed Himself to be the Primal Point around which "the realities of the Prophets and Messengers revolve."[8] I needed the answer to the question "What hath God wrought?"

The seed that bears the fruit of the story behind the quote of Numbers 23:23 was Cain's jealousy of his brother Abel. That jealousy sprouted, feeding on God's promises to Abraham. It put down roots in Sarah's desire to cast out Abraham's son Ishmael in favor of her son Isaac, and the trunk of the tree is the deceitfulness of Jacob, the heel catcher later known as Israel, toward his brother Esau. The twisted branches of the tree are formed by the rivalry among Jacob's twelve sons.

Ten of these sold their brother Joseph into slavery in Egypt, and Joseph later rescued them from famine. They all became enslaved, and eventually the twelve tribes of Israel were freed from that slavery and wandered aimlessly, rather than circumambulating, for forty years in the desert, during which an entire generation died. The story then brings us to God's assistance to their children, as they continued to stumble their way ahead, two repentant steps forward, followed by one more sinful step back, in their efforts to conquer the promised land. Despite their failings, the nations around them begin to understand that they had supernatural backing.

Numbers 22 finds the conquering Israelites camping in the plain of Moab by Jericho, east of the river Jordan. We learn that Moab was distressed because of the children of Israel, and the King of Moab, a man named Balak, teamed up with Midian to hire a prophet to curse Israel. The prophet's name was Balaam.[9]

Balaam seeks permission from God to curse the Israelites but is told that God is blessing them. Hilarity ensues, as this greedy prophet seeks a way around God's explicit boundaries. Balaam dances in and out between the increasing pressure from and the rewards offered by the regional royalty in exchange for one little favor—a curse on Israel. The famous story of Balaam's ass—in which God speaks to this prophet through his donkey—is part of the narrative. In the end, God allows Balaam to go with the men, but under strict orders only to pronounce that which God allows him to say.[10]

---

8 Shoghi Effendi, *God Passes By* (Wilmette: Bahá'í Publishing Trust, 1971), 57.
9 Numbers 22:1-7.
10 Numbers 22:8-41.

Numbers 23 opens with Balaam asking Balak to build seven altars on a mountaintop and sacrifice animals on each. Perhaps by forcing Moab's king to worship God, Balaam hopes to ingratiate God to both Balak and himself and gain permission to pronounce a wee little curse against Israel, destined to make him rich.[11]

God actually seems to accommodate this, to a degree. Balaam, who clearly conveys that he is not allowed to curse or denounce anyone whom God has not cursed or denounced, delivers a "live and let live" pronouncement that establishes Israel as a nation, apart from the others: "For from the top of the rocks I see him, and from the hills I behold him: lo, the people shall dwell alone, and shall not be reckoned among the nations."[12]

This certainly seems to mirror the first fifty years of Israel's modern existence. She has clearly been protected, while also behaving with great restraint. Israel stood apart, not joining the nuclear nonproliferation treaty but ensuring that she had the means to protect herself. Many nations in the world are just like Balak in this story, very upset with this. He wants a curse. He does not want to live apart, in peace. He wants Israel gone.

So Balak tries again. Another mountain is chosen, another seven altars are built, and Balaam again disappoints him by pronouncing a blessing on Israel. Only, this time God's message is more pronounced and final, including "God is not a man, that he should lie" and "he hath blessed; and I cannot reverse it." Perhaps most importantly in this context is this: "He hath not beheld iniquity in Jacob, neither hath he seen perverseness in Israel: the LORD his God is with him, and the shout of a king is among them."[13]

Looking back at the last few decades, Israel has shown that the Jewish state is here to stay, no matter how much hatred and animosity is stirred up against it. And even as Israel continues to demonstrate "what hath God wrought," there has arisen an unbelievable hypocrisy—a lie—about who and what Israel and the Jews really are, and a denial of her right to exist at all. This denial extends to her heritage in the land, the holy sites that constitute her history, her right to self-determination, including establishing a capital how and where she wants.

God then and now declares that He is not a man and will not participate in a lie nor break His promise to Israel.

The Bible is explicit in revealing Israel's many sins, for which God explicitly pronounced punishment on them. And though they did not originally have a king, they would be chastened later for wanting one. Yet God emphasizes

11 Numbers 23:1-4.
12 Numbers 23:9.
13 Numbers 23:13-21.

that He has chosen this people, in the context of their pending entry into the promised land, which would occur when they crossed over the river Jordan. And there are many verses explaining that all these things happened to Israel specifically as a type, a forerunner, a prophetic pattern of events. Paul specifically relates these events to the end times.[14]

AND IN THE END

This brings us, in this prophetic story, at the juncture of a second attempt being made to levy a curse against Israel, to the verse referenced by that momentous quote used in the first-ever telegraph, May 24, 1844:

> Surely there is no enchantment against Jacob, neither is there any divination against Israel: according to this time it shall be said of Jacob and of Israel, What hath God wrought![15]

"According to this time" has also been translated as "from this day." When tied to the Edict of Toleration, the declaration of the Báb, the birth of 'Abdu'l-Bahá, the end of the times of the Gentiles, the prophesied arrival of the Twelfth Imam, and more, the evidence that this is no mere set of coincidences is striking. The astronomical clock was completely in sync with the atomic clock; the millennia outlined in the stars were calibrated to the infinitely perfect timing of the seconds ticking along on earth:

> Behold, the people shall rise up as a great lion, and lift up himself as a young lion: he shall not lie down until he eat of the prey, and drink the blood of the slain.[16]

Balak, whose name means "devastator," reacts with a backtracking statement: "Neither curse them at all, nor bless them at all." This is not surprising, given the direction in which things were trending. Israel was going to keep to themselves, but now, because of the effort to curse them, they would rise up like a great lion. And they would not stop until they had devoured their prey. Perhaps Balak was realizing that the more he determined to oppose this people, the more devastation he would bring upon himself.

---

14 1 Corinthians 10:11: "Now all these things happened unto them for examples: and they are written for our admonition, upon whom the ends of the world are come."
15 Numbers 23:23.
16 Numbers 23:24.

But Balak, like Pharaoh of old and others who, and despite the Edict of Toleration, the Balfour Declaration, and the UN Mandate for the establishment of the modern State of Israel, have mounted opposition against the right of Jews to establish a Nation in the Holy Land, decides to ignore God's clear statement that there could be no curse against her. And he persists in his efforts to bring a curse on Israel.

Another mountain is selected and again seven altars are built and sacrifices are offered. This time Balaam doesn't even ask God if he can curse Israel, as he knows the answer. Instead he falls into a trance and reemphasizes the message in Numbers 23:23, reiterating that Israel is a lion blessed of God, adding, for good measure, that those who bless Israel will be blessed, and those who curse her will be cursed.

Balak is angry that three blessings have now been pronounced, an important number in biblical terms. But this anger simply causes Balaam, through the end of chapter 23 and well into chapter 24, to shift focus away from blessing Israel to the fate of those who oppose her, concluding with a long list of all the tribes, peoples, and nations that will be destroyed by Israel. And Balaam's introduction to this detailed prophecy of future conquest leaves no doubt about the fact that its actual fulfillment was not for that time at all: "And now, behold, I go unto my people: come therefore, and I will advertise thee what this people shall do to thy people in the latter days."[17] The term "latter days" is used to designate the end times.

In verse 17 we read, "I shall see him, but not now: I shall behold him, but not nigh: there shall come a Star out of Jacob." This calls out the prophetic nature of the passage—that what Balaam saw was not for that time, but for a time in the distant future. And indeed this came true. Nazi Germany used what we know today as the "Star of David" to identify the Jews, in their effort to completely exterminate them. The Holocaust, however, also drove large numbers of persecuted survivors—and others who began to understand that they stood at a unique juncture in history—to the Holy Land to establish modern Israel. And today that prophesied star out of Jacob, the Star of David, graces the Israeli flag. Like a homing bird across space-time, they landed, home and dry.

The verse continues, "And a Sceptre shall rise out of Israel, and shall smite the corners of Moab, and destroy all the children of Sheth." These two nations are but two of the peoples listed here, who are prophesied to be crushed by Israel in the future. The Hebrew word for sceptre here is *shebet*, "rod."

---

17 Numbers 24:14.

It is the same word David used in Psalm 2:9: "Thou shalt break them with a rod of iron; thou shalt dash them in pieces like a potter's vessel." Psalms 2:9 is quoted in Revelation 2, and the phrase "rod of iron" is then repeated twice later in that book.

The phrase the "rod of iron" signifies the return of Christ in power and His forceful imposition of authority over the nations. This connection lent new significance to Israel's role with regard to the ensign to the nations. At Christ's return, great destruction would come upon humankind, bringing them into submission to this rod of iron, which would otherwise "dash them in pieces like a potter's vessel."

Ever-Present Past

Some things are so unexpected that no one is prepared for them.
—Leo Rosten

Balaam declared that his prophecy was intended for the end of days. My position is that there is a dual fulfillment, that which happened prior to Christ and that which was to happen at the time of His second coming and the "great and terrible day of the LORD."[1] And while locking down the specific identity of the ten or more city-states Balaam calls out for destruction by Israel in the end time would be tedious, it's pretty clear, generally, that they are Israel's neighbors in the Middle East. They are, therefore, the nations currently intent on bringing a curse on Israel. Strikingly, these nations are under the sway of either Sunni or Shia Islam. Is it a coincidence that these nations cover the geography governed by the Umayyads, identified by 'Abdu'l-Bahá as the Beast? We would do well to consider these facts and ask ourselves what may yet be ahead of us.

Subsequent end-time prophecies ratchet this up, implicating much more expansive geographies and much greater numbers of people. Broad-based destruction is prophesied in the aforementioned day of the Lord, which is but a part of the "the great tribulation."[2] Balaam sums it up like this in Numbers 24:23: "Alas, who shall live when God doeth this!"

Who indeed?

---

1 Joel 2:11, 31.
2 Matthew 24:21-22: "For then shall be great tribulation, such as was not since the beginning of the world to this time, no, nor ever shall be. And except those days should be shortened, there should no flesh be saved: but for the elect's sake those days shall be shortened."

THE NIGHT BEFORE

It's time to bring up another fascinating thread opened up by my interest in the Bahá'í faith. The connection between the scattering at Babel and the meaning of the Báb's declaration—as the Gate of God through which humankind would be brought together—seemed to me to represent a complete circle. God had stated that "now nothing will be restrained from them, which they have imagined to do."[3] What they had imagined to do was build a tower to heaven. What occupied my thinking in trying to put all this together was that if there was any validity to the Bahá'í view of God and religion, then the confusion at Bab El was about more than not being able to talk with one another. Different segments of humanity held different intellectual, emotional, and spiritual capacities, and great human endeavors needed these combined contributions.

The clue needed to put these puzzle pieces together might be right under my nose, but I had ignored it because of my arrogant bias about being a person of the Sign. Opening my eyes to this possibility was a bittersweet and tantalizing prospect. Hinduism, Buddhism, and Islam were no less corrupt, I was sure, than I knew orthodox Christianity to be. I had spent decades peeling away at that onion, but I knew little about the other world religions. At the same time, I didn't see why God wouldn't give answers to anyone who was diligently knocking at this door. It was time to throw caution to the wind with regard to the perspectives the Bahá'í Faith was offering and start actively digging into this fertile new soil.

One clue had already pointed me in the direction of an important heavenly sign. In talking about the unity of religions, Bahá'ís had mentioned the idea that the magi who visited Christ in Bethlehem were Zoroastrian priests. This caught my attention, because the story of the magi visiting Christ had never made sense from my myopic perspective of God as the God of the Bible alone. Did the Bible actually support the idea that the cross-pollination of religions might be a positive thing?

I looked into the history and origins of Zoroastrianism and saw the possibility of a Zoroastrian connection between Daniel and Nebuchadnezzar's astrologers (who would have been Zoroastrian priests) who couldn't interpret the king's dreams. Daniel had been given a book—the book that outlined prophecies that led to 1844. God had sealed up the book and told Daniel, "Go thy way, Daniel: for the words are closed up and sealed till the time of the end. Many shall be purified, and made white, and tried; but the wicked shall do wickedly: and none

---

3 Genesis 11:6.

of the wicked shall understand; but the wise shall understand."[4] Wise men, or magi, from the East had then followed Christ's star.

Was it possible that the king's astrologers might have had access to Daniel's book, with or without his permission? And that they, having been upstaged by Daniel in front of the king, would have had more than a passing interest in Daniel's prophecies? And that these amazing sealed prophecies might have correlated to their own prophecies in such a way that they had enough puzzle pieces between these inputs to understand what was sealed?

My little sister, who had studied astrology, once explained to me that you created an astrological birth chart by knowing the time and the location of a birth. What if, I wondered, Zoroastrian priests, under Nebuchadnezzar, knowing that Daniel had access to God, from having seen him in action, had correlated Daniel's writings with signs in the heavens, using time and location to track down Christ at His first coming? While my path to it was different, a little online research provided adequate evidence that I wasn't the first one to have made the connection, and others had documented the heavenly signs the wise men had followed, to their— and now my—satisfaction.[5]

DARK HORSE

There were also numerous references in Bahá'í writings to the impor- tance of the indigenous peoples of the planet. Through the colonization of the great powers and the spread of dominant civilizations many tribes and nations had been persecuted, slaughtered, subjugated, pushed aside, and in many cases almost exterminated. Bahá'ís viewed them as an important factor in the end-time fulfillment of prophecies initiated by the arrival of the Gate of God.

As I opened my mind to the idea the Bahá'í writings held important keys to understanding, I felt that ancient cultures might have carried forward pieces of what was needed to build a tower to heaven. When I looked into this some- thing fascinating quickly became apparent. They all seemed not only to have a creation story (which made sense, since we all want to know where we came from) but also all shared eerily similar eschatological stories (prophecies about the end times).

One of the most striking was "The Legend of Turtle Island" as shared with me in a group on LinkedIn (a large professionally-oriented social media website)

---

4 Daniel 12:9-10.
5 Chad Ashby, "Magi, Wise Men, or Kings? It's Complicated," Christianity Today, December 16, 2016, http://www. christianitytoday.com/history/holidays/christmas/magi-wise-men-or-kings-its-complicated.html.

by Abe Walking Bear Sanchez. He said Jack Brightnose Sr., a Cree medicine man, told it to him. I've reproduced it below.

Long ago when animals talked and people did not, all people lived on Turtle Island. Each, while different was the same.

The Creator came to Turtle Island and said to the people: You are to divide into groups and go off in different directions. Each group will go through the cycles of time apart from the others.

There will come a time when you will come back together, form the sacred circle and share what you've learned while apart, and there will be a time of cooperation, peace and prosperity.

The group that went off to the East became known as the red race and the medicine wheel is painted red on that side. This group was given care of Mother Earth and all the animals and plants found there.

The group that went off to the South became known as the yellow race and the medicine wheel is painted yellow at the bottom. This group was given care of the air and all the birds found there.

The group that went off to the West became known as the black race and the medicine wheel is painted black on that side. This group was given care of the waters and the seas and all life found there.

The group that went off to the North became known as the white race, and the medicine wheel is painted white at the top. This group was given care of fire, which in time became mathematics and science.

Each group was given the additional responsibility of remembering in their hearts that all men are brothers, that there is but one race.

While going through the cycles of time apart, the people learned to speak each in their own way, and in so doing they almost forgot that they had once all been alike. Many came to think of each other as strangers.

We've learned much while apart and as the Creator promised, we are sharing what we've learned. In so doing, we're coming back together. We're remembering who we are.

Those who would keep us apart have yet to learn that neither heat nor light is lost from sharing the camp fire. That when all people join the sacred circle we will have returned to Turtle Island and there will be Peace and Prosperity. As our Lakota Brothers say: "Mitakuye Oyasin" (We are all relatives).

Before I take the next step, which is a small step from here and a giant leap forward in my understanding of the Tower of Babel story, I need to spend at least one section in this chapter on what was happening on the ground.

YOU LIKE ME TOO MUCH

Following Angela's lead, at a safe distance, I was learning much from the Bahá'í Faith while checking everything against the Bible. I now thoroughly enjoyed Bahá'í prayer meetings, or devotional gatherings, as they called them, though they had initially been mildly uncomfortable for me. I loved the prayers and quotes from multiple religions, the diverse, inspiring music, but especially the open discussions I had with people of different spiritual perspectives. I always learned something that led to one more step forward in pursuit of the answers to my questions.

Exactly how would God address the confusion of these now corrupt religions? What was the exact role that Israel would play? How and when would Christ actually bring about the long-awaited Kingdom of God?

When Angela wanted me to join her in a formal course covering the doctrines of the Bahá'í faith, however, I became nervous. Hanju, a woman of culture and grace from Korea, whose international experience included involvement at the United Nations had invited Angela to join a "Ruhi Group." Ruhi, in 2006, was a relatively new series of facilitated sessions covering the basic tenets and history of the Bahá'í faith. It incorporated the principle of Bahá'í consultation, while attempting to accelerate the process of reaching agreement by inserting a tutor who systematically covered specific topics through a series of courses.

It wasn't that I was worried about being indoctrinated; it was more of a two-edged sword. I wasn't worried about compromising on what I knew to be true; I just didn't want to be put in a position of having to argue with anyone about the inevitable difference of opinion with which we would be confronted. And even more so, I didn't want to end up on the other side of an important belief from Angela.

The second edge of the sword was subtler, and it surprised me as I became aware of my feelings about it. I really didn't want to see the Bahá'í Faith degrade itself by revealing that, despite all the protestations to the contrary and its own teachings about the independent investigation of truth, it was engaged in indoctrination. These were the thoughts I had as we drove up to the house of a lovely couple where the class was held.

I was pleasantly surprised to see that the group consisted of mostly non-Bahá'ís, from a variety of backgrounds and languages. Hanju had also gone to extraordinary effort to make us feel comfortable and welcome, providing an amazing spread of healthy, organic, and homemade snacks, along with Persian tea brewing in a Turkish samovar.

But as we completed our introductions and small talk and sat down in front of our notebook-sized Ruhi books, I spent a few moments examining the warm, red cover. At the top was the image of a silhouetted man seeming to walk briskly to join a line of multicultural, multigenerational figures holding hands. Below this were color photos of small, diverse groups studying or listening intently. The photos reminded me of WCG promotional materials and those distributed by Jehovah's Witnesses and other groups intent on the conversion of others. This reignited my fears that this was nothing but a thinly veiled indoctrination program.

My fears were somewhat alleviated as we covered the introductory section called "To the Collaborators." Although there was "an experienced person who acts as a tutor," the book put the word "students" in quotation marks and described the process as one in which everyone learns. My heart sank again, though, as we began the first section, titled "Understanding the Bahá'í Writings." It was, quite literally, exactly the format used in the infamous Ambassador College correspondence course. For those unfamiliar with that effective tool deployed by the WCG, I'll take a moment to explain.

Section 1 of the Ruhi book opens with a short paragraph: "In this unit you will study short passages from the Writings of the Faith and think about how you can apply them to your life." It explained how the "students" would take turns posing and answering the questions and encouraged memorization of these passages from the Bahá'í writings that would be used. And then it presented a series of five short quotes and questions, starting with this one: "The betterment of the world can be accomplished through pure and goodly deeds, through commendable and seemly conduct."[6] The question posed after this quote was "How can 'the betterment of the world be accomplished'?" with a space in which we dutifully wrote down, "Through pure and goodly deeds, through commendable and seemly conduct."

Being told to memorize quotations by rote, in spoon-fed chunks, through the use of questions that aren't really questions, brought back bad memories. This is how indoctrination in the teachings of the WCG, many of which had later proven to be incorrect, had been administered. It would not be an exaggeration to state that this grieved the life of my spirit, at that moment.

Accordingly, I will somewhat sheepishly admit I determined to do my best to force Hanju to prove that she really believed in the opening statement about reciprocal learning, as well as the idea that the Bible was the Word of God, along with the Bahá'í writings. As we moved on to sections on prayer and life and death, I would repeatedly try Hanju's patience, as well as introduce more quotes from the Bible than anyone in the group had bargained for. To her credit, she proved to me that her respect for the beliefs of others was genuine, and when she did, from time to time, gently remind me that the purpose of the group was to learn about the Bahá'í writings, not the Bible, her kind admonishments were timely and appropriate.

And, amazingly, with the exception of the immortality of the soul, which WCG theology rejected, what the Bahá'í Faith taught about prayer, heaven, hell, and the Trinity, for example, was pretty much exactly what I had come to believe, based on my own study of the Bible. Even on the issue of the soul, the way in which the Bahá'í writings approached this topic left adequate room for interpretation. I revisited verses from Job, Proverbs, Ecclesiastes, and elsewhere about the spirit in or of humans and other relevant passages that had led me to a different conclusion. In the end, I was able to accept that the Bahá'í teachings on this subject were not in opposition to what the Bible said.

And there was an important positive takeaway. The Bahá'í definition of Manifestation of God, as applied to Jesus, solved the problem of understanding His nature in the light of the Bible's clear statements about God being One in a way that was superior to what I had heard anywhere else. This includes formulations about the Trinity and the various ways in which the WCG and other groups attempt to make statements on the nature of God. In my view, such convoluted positions mangled distinctions between Jesus and God as documented by the Bible's statements about God and the words of Jesus about Himself, whereas the Bahá'í formulation made sense to me.

---

6 Baha'u'llah, trans. by Shoghi Effendi, "Gleanings from the Writings of Baha'u'llah," (Bahá'í Publishing), 155-56.

I WANT YOU (SHE'S SO HEAVY)

The pace of our Ruhi I class was glacial, not only because of my constant need to compare what was being covered to the Bible, but because several of those who attended spoke very poor English. Almost every word of a religious nature needed to be defined, along with many others that would be familiar to a native speaker. Meanwhile, the big day for Angela and me was drawing near, even as a new wrinkle emerged.

As Angela was tightening up her orbit around the greater Los Angeles Bahá'í community, I, like the tide, was being pulled along with her. She was ready to declare as a Bahá'í—which means to confess acceptance that Bahá'u'lláh was who the Báb declared him to be: he whom God will make manifest, the Promised One of all ages, the Glory of God.

I wasn't.

This wasn't actually a problem for Angela or for Bahá'ís, but due to a simple twist of fate, it threatened our pending marriage.

As we discussed our desire to have a Bahá'í wedding with our friends, we learned about the law of consent. Bahá'ís wishing to marry must first gain permission from their parents, which, if withheld, will prevent them from marrying. I knew that my dad, if the responsibility of doing so were pressed upon him, would never be able to consent to his son marrying outside of his religion.

Angela and I decided to consult with Hanju's husband, who was a member of the Local Spiritual Assembly (LSA) of Bahá'ís in his community. He was quick to point out that individual members of the nine-member elected LSAs had no authority or special insight outside of that body. Any opinion he might provide was strictly his own, which carried no more weight than the opinion of anyone else. We affirmed that we understood and requested his opinion anyway.

He explained that Bahá'í laws are not considered binding outside the Bahá'í Faith and that unless and until we declared as Bahá'ís there was no need to concern ourselves with the Bahá'í faith's laws. This was music to my ears. I also appreciated yet another glimpse into the practical, level-headed, and detached approach to spiritual ideals and human reality which was always in evidence within this increasingly intriguing belief system. Angela and I quickly agreed to put off any further talk about declaring as Bahá'ís until after the wedding, but that didn't stop either of us from continuing to explore the Bahá'í faith.

What we had already learned together in our investigation of God, spirituality, religion, and each other, in light of the Bahá'í faith, both intellectually and in practice, had provided a solid foundation for a marriage built to last. The point of wanting a Bahá'í wedding wasn't to appear to be Bahá'ís, which we weren't, but rather to focus on the development of mature adult hearts, willingly submitting to God and one another.

And with regard to that Bahá'í wedding prayer, "We will all verily abide by the Will of God," we were both agreeing to submit to the light, to what God reveals, which made our choice of the moon and the tide as the theme of our wedding all the more magical.

And it was the moon, the lesser light, which proved to be the clue that would help me assemble all the pieces of the puzzle. It was the key that finally unlocked the mystery of the Tower of Babel that had ignited my curiosity, its connection to our modern age, and the arrival of the Báb.

HOPE OF DELIVERANCE

A Jewish tradition holds forth that in the beginning God filled every nook and cranny of nothingness. He was everywhere. He permeated all. There was nothing BUT God. To pursue His decision to create something—us and all that was necessary for us to survive—and to ultimately fulfill His purpose, He had to pull Himself back, gather up His Spirit-self, to make room for a creation.

From the very first, before space-time existed, before it unfolded and evolved to the point that the earth was created, before the gathering of red dirt into clay, before that first sin was committed against God, the covenant between God and Jesus was already made. The plan could not fail because God is perfect and failure with God is not possible. God didn't create us to destroy us. He created us to love us. And He created us so that He could be with us, to literally be IN us, so that we would find meaning, purpose, life, and yes, rest, in Him.

But for us to voluntarily return to that relationship, to turn fully to the light and circumambulate the divine, we were given the freedom to make our own choices, with all their imperfection. God created a space beneath the light, with a bit of sovereignty of its own, where such imperfection could exist. And a barrier was set at the bottom edge of that lesser light, above which these imperfections were not permitted.

And within that space, God restricted His presence, His Spirit, to obey our sovereignty. Only that which we consciously invite in is allowed. And when it is allowed, it pollinates, it germinates, and it brings forth new spirit life, and allows our spirit to soar heavenward. And our desire to do so is motivated by the structure of the universe, its fractal patterns—the way that particles and energy intermingle and aggregate up into orbits of attraction—that both punish us for our imperfections and motivate us to reach for the higher, the greater, the inspiring, the pure.

The freedom we have as humans is represented by the quantum particles, especially the electron, which has both a positive and a negative spin until such time as it is tested or observed, at which point the spin is fixed. The first Hidden Word of Bahá'u'lláh speaks of what is necessary for us to obtain the correct spin, the correct orientation.[7] A pure, kindly, and radiant heart enables the germination that can extend our sovereignty beyond the confines imposed by our physical nature, our subservience to the lesser light, the orb positioned at the exact border of our freedom. Put another way, within that space we are kings and queens, free to mature, with the light intended to illuminate the dark dungeon that is our ego, our desire to be separate and distinct from God.

It is only purity of heart that can free us from hell, which is separation from the light, separation from God.

In symbolic terms, at an individual level, we could talk now about a stairway to heaven, Jacob's ladder, the ascent of our souls. But I'm a fundamentalist at heart. This was not good enough for me. I took these stories too literally and was willing, like Majnun, to keep knocking on the door, to keep searching, until I had a satisfying answer.

Babel was humanity's aborted attempt to ascend to heaven on our own terms, apart from submission to God, to appropriate the name "the Gate of God," which God had in fact reserved for another time. Humanity, at the Tower of Babel—the point in time when it was of one language—was able to align on this goal, the effort to ascend beyond the limits imposed at creation. They did this, not because they were letting the light in or were bothered by the separation, but because they had shut it out and believed they were self-sufficient. They felt they had everything necessary to extend their sovereignty without permission, without invitation, to reach out and conquer. They built a city that laid claim to be the Gate of God and sought to raise a tower that would be an ensign to the nations, to all peoples, to gather together underneath its shadow.

This counterfeit false Sign was envisioned by those who felt they were independent of God and was intended to cause people to turn away from the light, to give up their sovereignty before God, to become enslaved by Babylon and its rulers.

God chose to call it what it was—confusion—and in confusing the language, to thwart the clarity of purpose, the power of their unity, which was being put

---

7 Bahá'u'lláh - *The Hidden Words*, Arabic no. 1.

to an evil purpose. God returned humanity to their allotted station and put a governor on their progress by making communication of the lie more difficult.

As humanity regrouped and rebuilt, they traversed the globe, overcame the language barriers, and developed civilizations capable of subduing vast reaches of the planet and the peoples on it. Divine messengers and prophets came to different peoples and at different times, to turn us back to the light. But each time the resulting positive growth was deployed to force others to bend to the superior power of whoever was in control of the resources and could apply them to dominion and subjection, enslaving and ruling over their brothers and sisters. These waves of dominion and control are what has led to the system of systems defined and described in Revelation under the label "Babylon the Great."

Since 1844, and 1948, we have taken over the entirety of the arena available to us, right up to and including that barrier in the sky that marks the boundary between heaven and earth—the lesser light. And we again have begun extending our feelers beyond it.

LONG, LONG, LONG

During this same time the plan of God has also reached maturity. A new era was introduced at the declaration of the Báb—the Gate of God—and the end of the times of the Gentiles. The training wheels and the governors were taken off humankind's progress and the spiritual understanding that has germinated as humanity allowed the light to bear fruit in us has given rise to cooperative forms of government that harnessed the potential of humankind in new ways for this day and age. This includes the arrival of democracy and the establishment of the federalist system of the United States of America.

This "New World" attracted people from all segments of all societies and granted them equality and opportunity in a way never seen before in the history of humankind. With the Emancipation Proclamation in 1863, the course was firmly set for the unlimited potential of this melting pot to unfold.[8] The separation that occurred at the Tower of Babel was undone. Now nothing would be restrained from us which we imagined to do. The year 1863 is (coincidentally?) the year in which Bahá'u'lláh declared himself to be the Promised One of all ages.

As the mind-blowing implications of these connections sank in, I had to backtrack to understand just how unbelievably intricate is the weave of God's hand, to even begin to grasp the unfathomable magnitude of what God had wrought.

---

8 The proclamation declared "that all persons held as slaves" within the rebellious states "are, and henceforward shall be free."

Bahá'u'lláh, proclaimed that "the Great Republic of the West" would lead the world to the Most Great Peace. At the same time, the first Bahá'í temple, which I had begun to see as the plan and method by which the Kingdom of God, Bahá'í style, was to be rolled out across the planet, was, established in Ashgabat, Turkmenistan.

The first Bahá'í House of Worship was built in the city of 'Ishqábád. It was begun in 1902 and completed in 1908. 'Ishqábád is located in the desert plain of western Turkmenistan near the foothills of the Alborz Mountains. Under the protection and freedom given by the Russian authorities, the number of Bahá'ís there rose to over one thousand, and for the first time anywhere in the world, a true Bahá'í community was established. Eventually the Bahá'ís in 'Ishqábád decided to build the institution of the spiritual and social heart of the Bahá'í community: the Mashriqu'l-Adhkár. The translation of this is "the dawning place of the mention of God."

The House of Worship itself was surrounded by gardens. At the four corners of the garden were four buildings: a school, a hostel where travelling Bahá'ís were entertained, a small hospital, and a building for groundskeepers. The Bahá'ís lived as much as possible in proximity to the House of Worship. It was the center of the community physically, as well as spiritually. The House of Worship in 'Ishqábád has been the only House of Worship thus far to have the humanitarian subsidiaries associated with the institution built alongside it.

After serving the community for two decades, the House of Worship was expropriated by the Soviet authorities in 1928 and leased back to the Bahá'ís. This lasted until 1938, when it was fully secularized and turned into an art gallery. The 1948 Ashgabat earthquake seriously damaged the building and rendered it unsafe; the heavy rains of the following years weakened the structure. It was demolished in 1963 and the site converted into a public park.

One of the many questions I had about the Bahá'í Faith at that time, which allowed me to circumambulate it at a fair distance, was this: if it was what it claimed to be, the arrival of the Kingdom of God on earth, or at least the developing embryo of it, then why would God allow its first temple to be destroyed? That did not remotely align with a return of Christ carrying a rod of iron to subdue the nations.

Now, the following section on Russia and America, in particular, is personal speculation and interpretation, but the answer to this question which I intuited from my research of these coincidences satisfied me, and I share it in the spirit of fascinating speculation that may or may not prove to be true.

God gave Russia a head start, for whatever reason, in the space race—the establishment of the tower to heaven. In this speculation, the extension of humanity's sovereignty beyond our planet is represented by and accompanied by the series of Bahá'í temples that were to be deployed across the planet, and which have only recently covered all inhabited continents. These form the physical representation of the Báb's station, the Gate of God, the Primal Point. Here are a few of the inputs into this perspective that led to me choosing the particular spin I'm putting on this set of electrons.

In 1844, while the Báb was declaring and 'Abdu'l-Bahá was being born and the first telegraph message was being sent, Karl Marx wrote, "Die Religion … ist das Opium des Volkes."[9] Lenin adopted this as a rallying cry, banning the "opiate of religion" from the newly born Soviet Union, which was established in 1922; this utopian model, as the US had done earlier, declared all men to be equal materially, in a "worker's paradise." Unlike in the US, belief in God was outlawed. This union of states thus refused to submit to the governance God had put in place with the greater and lesser light, even as the US enshrined in its Pledge of Allegiance that we were "one nation under God, with liberty and justice for all."

So, in the weave of human history, two alternate systems of global unification were presented: the United States of America and its counterpoint, the Soviet Union. The Soviet Union had an early lead in the space race, but by the time of the establishment of the State of Israel in 1948, the same year the earthquake damaged that first temple, the die was already cast. And in 1961, when President Kennedy announced the US initiative to go to the moon, the US temple in Wilmette had finally been dedicated. In 1963, the 100th anniversary of Bahá'u'lláh's declaration, the desecrated House of Worship in 'Ishqábád was destroyed, and the Universal House of Justice was established, the supreme body of the Bahá'í faith.

Note that this was not just the global house of justice. "Universal" indicates a system of law and justice that extends beyond the boundaries of our planet. Why do I mention this?

Because everything I've said about the sovereignty of humankind on earth, the fractal patterns of particles aggregating up into systems of circumambulating matter, giving rise to space-time, consciousness, and so much more now comes into play. As does the city of Bab El, our first efforts to extend our sovereignty beyond the boundaries granted us. And the way in which this effort was stymied by God.

The question I asked was "How high would that tower have to have been, to reach to heaven?" Well, God put the greater and lesser lights "in heaven."

---

9 "Karl Marx: Religion Is the Opium of the People," Age of the Sage, accessed May 11, 2018, http://www.age-of-the-sage.org/quotations/marx_opium_people.html.

The moon, in other words, at 238,900 miles high would seem to be the measure of it.

And remember how God said, "This they begin to do: and now nothing will be restrained from them, which they have imagined to do"?[10]

Well, in the "you really can't make this up" department, in 1969 the Beatles unveiled a composition that Lennon, not Lenin, had spearheaded. It was an infectious song titled "All You Need Is Love" to a melody that interwove the national anthems of a variety of nations. The Beatles performed it live while four hundred million viewers tuned in to watch Neil Armstrong take one small step that represented a giant leap for mankind.

There are many reasons I wove the music of the Beatles into the fabric of each chapter of this trilogy. It is an homage to a group of guys who wrote music that spoke to me powerfully in my childhood, but also to their accomplishments, the universality of their music, and perhaps most of all, the strange belief that arose at the height of Beatle-mania that the Beatles were sending out hidden messages in their music. This seemed fitting, given the subject matter of this trilogy. John Lennon's opening lyric to "All You Need Is Love" is an example of how one could read significance into their lyrics. How fitting, at a moon landing that symbolized humankind finally achieving that which God had once forbidden that his song opened with "there's nothing you can do that can't be done."[11]

The United States of America was allowed to do what Nimrod, Babylon, and the Soviet Union, were not. We had finally built a tower that reached to heaven. The step that Armstrong took was from a capsule sent from earth to the surface of the lesser light. This light had been hung up by God to rule over us, and it set a boundary on our sovereignty. God had stopped a humanity that had wanted to extend beyond it. What couldn't be done now could be. The boundary was also a prophetic Sign whose time had come.

Two simple things come to mind. First, the goal of *e pluribus unum*—"from many, one"—was different than what took place at Babel. Nimrod's desire was to turn large numbers of people away from the light, in order to enslave them to the purpose of the rulers. Here it was a few brave souls turning toward the light, seeking religious freedom, who came to this new land to build cities and then states. There it was an attempt to form a nation apart from God, for

---

10 Genesis 11:6.

11 For the record, pun intended, I had already written and published the first versions of the first two volumes of this trilogy, without having made a connection to the moon landing. That insight came when I was on a trip to India, in 2014, during a midnight jet-lagged prayer session. The insight forced a rewrite of the first two volumes, delaying by several years the completion of this one. The music of the Beatles, however, had already been woven into the fabric of this trilogy long before the insight came. Selah!

the purpose of bringing them under an enforced set of beliefs. Here it was an attempt to form one nation, under God. With liberty and justice for all.

In contemplating humanity's ascent to heaven, the throne of God, or at least its border, one more biblical reference seemed to jump out at me. The lesser light was humanity's boundary, a milestone in the aggregation of fractal patters of particles forming orbits within orbits. The strange opening chapter of Ezekiel's prophecy described a vision of the creatures that were part of some kind of an omnidirectional transportation system supporting the throne of God, on which he saw "the likeness of the glory of the LORD."[12] This is described as follows: "Their appearance and their work was as it were a wheel in the middle of a wheel."[13] Perhaps this was Ezekiel's way of describing some version of the view that we're privileged with, given our modern scientific understanding of orbits. And God certainly sits above the entirety of His creation, as represented by the universe.

---

12 Ezekiel 1:28.
13 Ezekiel 1:16.

Letting Go

It takes patience to appreciate domestic bliss; volatile spirits prefer unhappiness.
—GEORGE SANTAYANA

Various calendars have been devised throughout history, using lunar and solar elements and based on the seasonal changes brought about by the angle of the earth toward the sun and its orbit around it. The pyramids were an early effort to achieve a calibration of this celestial chronology that was unprecedented and unrivaled until Galileo, Copernicus, and Newton ushered in the Enlightenment. In more recent times, advances in astronomy and globalization are again bringing a more perfect calibration of the heavens into focus. Recent scientific efforts to discern the most primordial events in time rely on sending massive instruments into space, forming triangles of sensors across our solar system designed to triangulate faint gravity waves that originated close to the big bang. LIGO, for example, is a physics experiment, often referred to as an observatory, designed to detect and understand the origins of gravitational waves, bringing us ever closer to scientific clarity[1]. The perspective I was seeking, however, required looking back at the earliest records of Divine Revelation of another sort.

I CALL YOUR NAME

There are many eschatological prophecies scattered around the earth. Various peoples have held tenaciously to traditions from a culturally prehistoric

---

1 LIGO: Laser Interferometer Gravitational-Wave Observatory, LIGO Caltech, accessed June 29, 2018, https://www. ligo.caltech.edu/.

time frame. There were key patterns and areas of agreement, such as the Mayan and Cherokee calendars which focused on 2012, raising global awareness around the symbolic significance of 12/21/2012. This is reminiscent of the way in which the Jews have retained the Sign given to them by Moses. I was discovering fascinating coincidences and connections in the amazing story that began with God letting humankind know that He and He alone would determine who and what would bear the name "Gate of God."

The moon landing itself is the focal point of an ancient prophecy. This prophecy was delivered to people who originally populated the soil upon which the tower to heaven was built, American Indians and Eskimos. The following is from a talk given by Lee Brown, formerly coordinator of the Indigenous Doctoral Program in the Department of Educational Studies at The University of British Columbia:

"You're going to see a time when the eagle will fly its highest in the night and it will land upon the moon." …"And at that time," they say, "Many of the Native people will be sleeping," which symbolically means they have lost their teachings. There are some tribes that say it will be as if they are frozen: they've been through the long winter.

But they say, "When the eagle flies [its] highest in the night, that will be the first light of a new day. That will be the first thawing of spring." Of course, at the first light of a new day, if you've stayed up all night, you notice it's really dark. And the first light, you want to see it, but you can't. It sneaks up on you. You want to see it change but it's dark and then pretty soon it's getting light before you know it.

The Eagle has landed on the moon, 1969. When that spaceship landed they sent back the message, "The Eagle has landed." Traditionally, Native people from clear up in the Inuit region, they have shared with us this prophecy, clear down to the Quechuas in South America. They shared with us that they have this prophecy. When they heard those first words, "The Eagle has landed," they knew that was the start of a new time and a new power for Native people. There was absolutely nothing strong before us now. We may do anything we wish.

In 1776 when the United States Government printed the dollar, in one claw [of the eagle], if you've ever noticed, there is an olive branch in this claw. They said that represented peace. The Indian elders shared with me in South Dakota that to them that represents the enslavement of black people.

In the prophecies of the Six Nations people they say there will be two great uprisings by black people to free themselves. We've seen one about 1964. There will be a second, more violent one to come. I'll get back to what that means in a minute. In the other claw is 13 arrows. The founding fathers of the United States said that represents the 13 States. But the elders say that represents the enslavement of the Native people.

When the Eagle landed on the moon, they decided to print a special silver dollar to commemorate that. … The original design showed the spaceship landing on the moon but at the last minute it was changed to an actual eagle. And in the eagle's claws is the olive branch, but the arrows are gone. The elders said, "That's our prophecy, we have been released." …

We're in that time now. We're between the first light of a new day and the sunrise. The sunrise is about to come and when it comes up everyone is going to see it. …

Within seven days of the time the Eagle landed on the moon, the Freedom of Indian Religion Act was introduced into the United States Congress. The legislation was introduced in 1969, less than seven days after the Eagle landed on the moon. Eventually it was passed in November of 1978, signed by President Carter. These are the physical manifestations of the spiritual prophecies that we have.[2]

MAYBE I'M AMAZED

I believe that beginning in 1844 the separation that began at Babel was reversed, in connection with prophetic announcements of the arrival of the Kingdom of God. Freedom was on the march, and enslaved peoples everywhere were being liberated. Though progress has come in fits and starts—two steps forward, one step back—humanity's attention has been on such issues in a new way.

From this perspective, I began to accept that, in opposition to the prophetic framework I had previously adopted—in which Christ would dramatically return and immediately shatter the fortresses of those in control—the global community was moving more organically toward the kind of unity forecast by the Bahá'ís. The establishment of the State of Israel was intended as the most visible component, due to the nature of the Jews being "the People of the Sign" but this ingathering into the Kingdom of God was happening across all peoples and all religions. Humanity was all beginning to see their own teachings, their own prophecies, in the light that was being slowly disseminated by the arrival of a new dawn.

2 Lee Brown (talk, Continental Indigenous Council, Tanana Valley Fairgrounds, Fairbanks, Alaska, 1986), http://www.ausbcomp.com/redman/hopi_prophecy.htm.

In Isaiah 40:5, the statement about the glory of the Lord being revealed was interrupted by a voice asking, "What shall I cry?" Herbert Armstrong believed himself to be that voice, a voice crying in the wilderness. But he derived the primary authority and his approach from Isaiah 58.[3]

He believed he had been raised up to specifically trumpet the "End-Time Warning Message" to the house of Jacob, which he claimed was the US and Great Britain. He had even penned and published a book titled *A Voice Cries Out* to document his claim. Isaiah 58:1 provides the definitive quote used in this claim, "Cry aloud, spare not, lift up thy voice like a trumpet, and shew my people their transgression, and the house of Jacob their sins."

The section continues with a call to change the approach of seeking God, through prayer and fasting, with the intent of helping or saving oneself and turning that focus toward others, as outlined in verse 6: "Is not this the fast that I have chosen? to loose the bands of wickedness, to undo the heavy burdens, and to let the oppressed go free, and that ye break every yoke?" These verses now resonated with me in the context of these American Indian prophecies. They were related to the United States being a liberating melting pot with the proven potential to unite the diverse elements of humankind in a positive pursuit of the age-old quest to build a stairway to heaven. If this doesn't yet gel for you, stick with me for a moment.

Verses 7-10 of Isaiah 58 define the focus and behaviors that lead to such ascendancy, such as sovereignty:

> Is it not to deal thy bread to the hungry, and that thou bring the poor that are cast out to thy house? when thou seest the naked, that thou cover him; and that thou hide not thyself from thine own flesh? Then shall thy light break forth as the morning, and thine health shall spring forth speedily: and thy righteousness shall go before thee; the glory of the LORD shall be thy reward. Then shalt thou call, and the LORD shall answer; thou shalt cry, and he shall say, Here I am. If thou take away from the midst of thee the yoke, the putting forth of the finger, and speaking vanity; and if thou draw out thy soul to the hungry, and satisfy the afflicted soul; then shall thy light rise in obscurity, and thy darkness be as the noon day.

I'LL CRY INSTEAD

This section of Isaiah 58 had always been one of my favorite passages. I had an intense attraction to the image of an iconoclastic voice crying out—calling

---

3 I've included the full text of Isaiah chapter 58 as Appendix 3.

for the loosening of the bonds of wickedness and the breaking of every yoke, ushering in a global era in which greed, corruption, and oppression would be replaced by love and kindness. The WCG had styled itself as the "Voice Crying Out" while only paying lip service to the message of the voice, failing to act as a sheep, but instead as a goat.

The conclusion of Isaiah chapter 58 was a primary reason I was so insistent, for so long, on holding on to the Sign of the Mosaic covenant—the Sabbath. Who wouldn't want to be invited to assist Christ, at His return, in accomplishing that which was prophesied in verses 11-12? "And the LORD shall guide thee continually, and satisfy thy soul in drought, and make fat thy bones: and thou shalt be like a watered garden, and like a spring of water, whose waters fail not. And they that shall be of thee shall build the old waste places: thou shalt raise up the foundations of many generations; and thou shalt be called, The repairer of the breach, The restorer of paths to dwell in."

Up until now I had read some of the formal Writings of the Bahá'íFaith, including the Writings of the Báb (the Gate of God) and 'Abdu'l-Bahá (the Servant of the Glory) and the Universal House of Justice, along with a few books by Bahá'í writers. But I had consciously avoided reading the writings of Bahá'u'lláh, (the Glory of God). I was avoiding His words altogether, and any formal intellectual evaluation of the claims I assumed were contained therein. My fear was that I would end up rejecting them. I had not wanted to create a rift between me and Angela, whom I dearly loved and needed in my life, or between me and the Bahá'ís, whom I was growing to love and wanted in my life.

I enjoyed what 'Abdu'l-Bahá wrote; it seemed familiar to the kinder, gentler passages of Jesus, those dealing with love, forgiveness, and acceptance. These kinds of attitudes seemed to be a primary reason Bahá'ís fulfilled the Sign of the Christian covenant—unconditional love to all humanity. And 'Abdu'l-Bahá also gave explanations of various Bible passages which made complete sense. The ones I had read, in a summary of lectures He had given in Paris called "Paris Talks," for example, generally didn't address questions or concerns I had, but I appreciated His welcoming approach in expounding His message to a largely Christian audience.

But the passages and prayers contributed by the Báb spoke to me most clearly and powerfully. The language used evoked both the covenants of Moses and Christ, along with the sense of history conveyed by Noah and Abraham and Israel's time in Egypt. There was an intense expectation of the imminence of Christ's return and of our need to purify ourselves in preparation. These words tapped into the core of my spiritual understanding and the reason I had devoted my life to preparing for that return. A quote I became aware of in writing this book sums up the attitude I had at this point, and my eagerness to rededicate my entire life and being to God again, wherever He might be leading me:

> The days when idle worship was deemed sufficient are ended. The time is come when naught but the purest motive, supported by deeds of stainless purity, can ascend to the throne of the Most High and be acceptable unto Him. [4]

This quote addressed exactly what Isaiah was getting at in chapter 58, a call to cast off the trappings of idle worship in favor of doing something to really help our fellow man. And it also summarizes the aggregation of data points I had been collecting on the Bahá'í Faith, and the way in which the dots were being connected and the stars were aligning forced me inexorably closer to acknowledging that the Bahá'í Faith was essentially correct in its entire approach and focus. It had a legitimate claim to be fulfilling these verses.

And in an amazing way, the next few verses of Isaiah 58 provided the most compelling evidence of all to me, that this new religion might possibly represent the day star, the light dawning out of obscurity and slowly expanding into the brilliance of the sun at noon.

Verses 13-14 tied the arrival of the Kingdom of God to the Sign of the Sabbath. "If thou turn away thy foot from the sabbath, from doing thy pleasure on my holy day; and call the sabbath a delight, the holy of the LORD, honourable; and shalt honour him, not doing thine own ways, nor finding thine own pleasure, nor speaking thine own words: then shalt thou delight thyself in the LORD; and I will cause thee to ride upon the high places of the earth, and feed thee with the heritage of Jacob thy father: for the mouth of the LORD hath spoken it."

I had thought, as part of the WCG, that our keeping of the Sabbath was instrumental, that we were being prepared to usher in the return of Christ and the fulfillment of all these things. That fantasy had blown up in 1995, with no alternative answer visible to me. I was unaware, for example, that on October 23, 1995, while I was on the flight from Hawaii to the mainland (described at the conclusion of *The People of the Sign*), as I looked out at the stars, asking God for a sign, a minor sign was in fact given.

On that day, some forty-seven years after the declaration of statehood in 1948, the Jerusalem Embassy Act, was passed by the 104th Congress on October 23, 1995. It was adopted with full bipartisan support by the Senate (93–5) and the House (374–37). The act became law without a presidential

---

4 From the Bab's "Address to the Letters of the Living." For those who would like to read a larger sampling the address is included in its entirety as Appendix 2.

signature on November 8, 1995. The act recognized Jerusalem as the capital of the State of Israel and called for Jerusalem to remain an undivided city.

The most recent development, at the time of finalizing this for publication, is the recognition by the United States of Jerusalem as Israel's capital, coinciding with its seventy-year anniversary as a nation, and fifty years since surviving the 1967 attempt to destroy it.

The lightning message in 1844, and its rhetorical prophetic question "What hath God wrought?" focuses our attention on those who were keeping the Sabbath, the Sign of the Mosaic covenant. The prophecy stated that "according to this time" curses against Israel would revert upon the one doing the cursing. The prophecy continues in verse 17 of Numbers 24 to declare, "I shall see him, but not now: I shall behold him, but not nigh: there shall come a Star out of Jacob, and a Sceptre shall rise out of Israel, and shall smite the corners of Moab, and destroy all the children of Sheth." This rod of iron was also to be applied to a host of other peoples, tribes, and nations.

Having come through the waters of Israel and the fiery furnace, and having fulfilled Isaiah 58, the Jewish state is now being fed with the heritage of Jacob. Now what?

PHOTOGRAPH

It's important to realize that the book of Revelation is like a movie trailer, covering the entire history of the world over the last two thousand years, with references going back into prehistory and on into the future, even from today's perspective. That is one reason why its verses don't always seem to match up to their fulfillment, because a process that might unfold over hundreds of years is represented by two sequential sentences that seem to be happening in immediate succession. Revelation 14 is a good example of this effect. In it there are references to many of the topics covered over the course of this trilogy, in a manner that seems to happen almost all at once. In fact, the events are likely spread out over hundreds of years.

As my wedding approached, I had begun to rearrange so much of my understanding based on the Bahá'í writings. I did not, at that time, have the coherent understanding of how the movie actually flowed, as represented in this volume. And yet I was at the point where I could no longer avoid the very obvious claim implied in the name Bahá'u'lláh, that the founder of the Bahá'í Faith was, in fact, the arrival of the Glory of God, the Promised One of all ages.

The possibility that Bahá'u'lláh might really be Who He claimed to be opened up a clear connection to the purpose of the true People of the Sign, the Jews, who had been gathered together in the Holy Land under divine protection. They were now empowered to overcome their enemies, who had not been content to let them dwell alone on that holy hill and who were, instead, bent on their destruction.

Bahá'u'lláh had been successively exiled and banished from Persia (known as Iran today) on a route that had led Him to a place the Persian authorities considered the armpit of the world at that time, Acre. Acre (also known as Acco and Akka) was then part of the Ottoman Empire. The Ottoman authorities cooperated with the Persians to send Bahá'u'lláh there because it was a prison city. It is situated on the northern end of what today is Israel, which didn't officially exist when Bahá'u'lláh was banished there.

The nation of Israel, which has largely been reclaimed from the desert and rebuilt upon the old waste places, is now home to the stunningly beautiful World Center of the Bahá'íFaith, surrounded by lush gardens, on Mount Carmel. Mount Carmel is the mountain on which Elijah had his famous showdown with the false prophets of Baal, to settle once and for all who God really was and who His people were.

This location was not due to some grand master plan on the part of the Báb, Bahá'u'lláh and 'Abdu'l-Bahá , scheming up a way to incorporate fulfilled prophecy into the fabric of a new religion. And yet there it is, conveniently located under the protection of an iron dome protecting those who prophetically possess a rod of iron, the Jews who form the nation of Israel, built by the reassembled scattered remnant of the Jews—the People of the Sign of the Mosaic covenant.

In the midst of this entire heady discovery, as I was trying to figure out if the quite literally unbelievable claims made by Bahá'u'lláh were true, I had a more pressing concern. I was the tide, following the moon. And the moon, Angela, had led me in the direction of orchestrating the greatest wedding ever known to man.

At least this man.

This day would eclipse my first wedding. It would be the most elaborately planned and meticulously executed wedding I had ever attended. A full year of preparations had gone into making sure every detail was perfect.

The ceremony was elaborately choreographed, with a variety of participants reading prayers and statements woven around musical components, which were intended to bring the religiously divergent audience together. The highlight was the vows which Angela and I had agreed to construct separately and to surprise each other with. We decided to follow these personal promises to each other with our pronouncement of the Bahá'í wedding vow, "We will all verily abide by the Will of God."

In the final month before the wedding, I had finished the work of putting together a keepsake for all in attendance—a musical memoir of the ceremony and the day, a CD featuring many original compositions by our musician friends who would perform at the wedding. This included prerecorded tracks from our harpist, performances planned for the ceremony by Devon and Nura Creitz, and compositions by my groomsman, Mark, who would perform dinner music. There were also a few ringers, such as Average White Band's "Cut the Cake," David Bowie's "Wedding Song" with its "Angel for Life" refrain, and Stevie Wonder's "I Believe (When I Fall in Love It Will Be Forever)," to which my angel and I practiced, in preparation for our first dance. It also secretly featured "The Moon and the Tide," which Devon and I had recorded. The CD cover featured an original black-and-white rendition of a full moon.

While the wedding preparations were successful beyond either of our expectations, my efforts to manage the wedding expenses had completely failed. The invitations, the venue, the decorations, the clothes, the travel, the food, accommodations, pre-dinner, post-brunch, DJ, cake, and more were all documented—in photos and video—by professionals highly recommended in the LA region, for whose services I mortgaged the future I was about to embark upon. (In true LA fashion, I only own the rights for noncommercial use, so you won't be seeing any of them in this book.)

All that aside, it was seventy-five degrees on March 31, 2007, at Hotel La Valencia, where clouds sheltered the outdoor guests from the sun, which only appeared as they parted on cue for me to kiss the bride, at which time it burst forth in approval of our union.

One event documented on the video was the signing of the wedding certificate by our fathers. Whether or not he might have withheld his consent if given the chance, my dad was caught on film giving it to the marriage. I apparently had something in common with Jacob, the heel catcher, who after purchasing the birthright from his brother Esau for a bowl of lentils, tricked his father Isaac, in his old age, into giving him the blessing he had intended for Esau.

And though we danced and celebrated into the wee hours, before we knew it the day we had been planning for over a year was over. The next thing we knew, we were off to Fiji, where we would celebrate our first week as a married couple. This was a leap into the unknown that I was all too happy to make. We were like two kids, running headlong off a cliff, jumping into the ocean below.

When we arrived, jet-lagged, we first had to take a local flight to a more remote part of the island. We boarded the tiny twin-engine plane and set off for our destination—an airport near the departure point to a semiprivate island. This island featured only two resorts, on opposite sides. Ours had just a few honeymoon cabins, centered around a common dining and meeting hall. Heaven for newlyweds.

Wind turbulence from a "weak tropical disturbance," however, soon threatened to force the plane back. Our fearless pilot soldiered on, though as the flight progressed the disturbance seemed to us to be anything but weak. When we landed, the flight was grounded, as it was announced that this tropical disturbance had been upgraded to a tropical storm. Unconcerned, we loaded into the ten-seater bus that was to take us to our boat.

Speaking for myself, a carefree honeymoon spirit was behind my enjoyment of the adventure of almost being washed away while crossing a small bridge overrun by water coming off a hill. The storm had begun to hit in earnest. When the driver stopped in the middle while the worst of a wave hit us, I opened the door to watch the water rushing over the bridge and just barely under the floor of the bus. Glancing over at Angela, I could see that she was not amused by the situation, nor by my opening of the door, which I dutifully and promptly shut.

Once across, we were at the shoreline in minutes, where we were told that the heavy waves were making it dangerous for the small outboard motor skiff sent to pick us up to reach the shore. We and our guides hoisted our bags above our heads and marched through knee-deep water, with waves surging to our chests, before reaching the anchored boat.

Once we clambered aboard, I took a photo of my terrified new bride, clinging to the other side of the boat, sure we would capsize. I was enjoying the thrill of it all, little realizing the danger we were actually in. Only later did we learn that the disturbance was upgraded to a cyclone as we were making the crossing. Cyclone Cliff, to be exact. The photograph is a reminder of exactly how little my new wife knew about the life she had signed up for in marrying me. And it reminds me of just how much of an angel she is for having done so.

A cyclone is a hurricane, but one that occurs in the southern hemisphere. The caretakers on our honeymoon island met us at the dock. Whisking us to the honeymoon cottage, they helped us batten down the hatches in preparation for the brunt of the storm. When we reemerged twenty-four hours later, we surveyed the damage, on our way to finally meet the others who would share the resort with us for the remainder of the week. A day later we met several couples who had been scheduled for the flight immediately after ours, which had been cancelled while we were in the air. I had managed to avoid being hit by yet another one of the numerous bullets I had dodged over the course of my tumultuous life. Despite all the turmoil I had known, now somehow my life just kept getting better and better.

WILD HONEY PIE

After our amazing newlywed withdrawal from civilization, we emerged to embark on a cruise around the Fiji Islands before flying to our final honeymoon destination, Tittirangi, outside Auckland, New Zealand. There we spent a wonderful week in a small cottage rented to us by a woman we had randomly met at a dinner in Pasadena, California. Jeff and Lisa Caudle were friends from my college days back in Pasadena, just minutes from the restaurant where we had met our new temporary landlord. They happened to be stationed in Auckland with the United Church of God. It turned out we were just minutes away from them, and they were our welcome party, lending us a car and generally making us feel special.

Tittirangi means "the fringe of heaven," and I was beginning to believe the Kingdom of God had indeed arrived.

Soon enough, unfortunately, the honeymoon ended. I'm reminded of one of my dad's favorite sayings: "After the honeymoon—then what?"

Indeed.

It was back to the reality of being an unpaid cofounder of an Internet start-up, with three young Bahá'ís who were barely out of college, funded largely by a portion of my life savings. I rented a midsized but very modern house on a hill in a wealthy section of town to celebrate my new life with Angela and also to represent GoHuman.com. This was important to accomplish what we were trying to do, which was to interest investors and other partners in the venture. Rent was $3,600 per month.

My head was in the clouds, and I eagerly worked and pitched the concept and managed the team and created and drove strategy and vision on how we would expand. Throughout the summer, things were looking good, even as I sold off some of my assets to pay the outstanding wedding and honeymoon bills and cover our growing monthly expenses.

Registrations on the site, however, proved elusive. There was no evidence of viral growth. Revenue from our operations and products continued to not materialize. Worst of all was how my partners didn't seem to care. They were confident it would eventually materialize, and they were living on shoestring budgets, renting a room in someone else's home, living with parents, or working a full-time job and doing GoHuman.com on the side.

I wasn't working anywhere else, and so I did have some spare time. Some of that was dedicated to proving, to my satisfaction, whether or not Bahá'u'lláh was Who and what He claimed to be.

There is a series of four imposing volumes written by a Persian follower of Bahá'u'lláh, titled *The Revelation of Bahá'u'lláh*. Paith, the young lady who had introduced Angela to the Bahá'í Faith, had given us a subsequent book by this author titled *The Covenant of Bahá'u'lláh*. At some point I picked it up and began to read.

Prior to reading this book, I had already accepted the Báb as a herald, announcing the return of Christ. The message proclaiming the imminent arrival of the Kingdom of God had gone forth by telegraph in 1844. That same day 'Abdu'l-Bahá was born, a perfect exemplar of the way of life taught by Christ. That he had called Christians to follow the disciples of Christ didn't hurt either.[5] But I still hadn't really come to grips with what this meant. After all, there was no reasonable alternative (if you accepted the Báb and what had begun in 1844 in the Holy Land) than to accept that Bahá'u'lláh was the One that the Báb had announced. And yet I was still holding back when it came to Bahá'u'lláh.

Working my way through the five hundred pages of this book was fascinating. Page after page reaffirmed everything I had learned throughout my life, even as it cast what I knew in a new light. It was an accurate, logical, and powerful narrative, clarifying many open questions and grey areas.

About one-third of the way through this weighty volume, I abruptly stopped reading.

A terrifying realization suddenly struck me like lightning.

Bahá'u'lláh was everything others believed about Him and more.

The impact of this understanding was so overwhelming that my heart began fibrillating as I lay on the couch reading.

There was no pain, but after a few seconds I began to feel weak. Ten seconds into this, even as my strength was draining, I realized the fibrillation wasn't going to stop. I stood up in the hope that changing the pull of gravity on my circulatory system might trigger a switch back to a normal heartbeat.

This didn't happen.

I walked slowly up the stairs, still trying to trigger a change in this terrifying condition.

---

5 'Abdu'l-Bahá: "But when they followed Christ and believed in Him, their ignorance gave place to understanding, cruelty was changed to justice, falsehood to truth, darkness into light. They had been worldly, they became spiritual and divine. They had been children of darkness, they became sons of God, they became saints! Strive therefore to follow in their steps, leaving all worldly things behind, and striving to attain to the Spiritual Kingdom." 'Abdu'l-Bahá, Paris Talks (Bahá'í Publishing, 2006), 33.

At the top of the stairs my heart was still twitching, so I lay down on the bed.

As it continued, I decided just to rest there until death overtook me.

I lay there for a while. It may have been five minutes or it might have been thirty. Eventually the fibrillation stopped. I continued to rest, as I felt my energy level slowly rise again.

As frightening as this experience was, after a short while, I rose from the bed and slowly walked back down the stairs.

There I lay down on the couch and began to read again.

By the time I had finished the book, I had accepted Bahá'u'lláh's claim of being "the Promised One of all ages."

Captain Hart stepped down from his spaceship—the search was over.

The book also provided adequate insight into how the covenant that Bahá'u'lláh brought had led to the establishment of an administrative order with the capacity to bring about the Kingdom of God on earth. This would unfold, over time, establishing the rule of the rod of iron—the Word of God— over the entire planet. It would work like yeast, like the growth of a mustard seed. But eventually the whole loaf of space-time would be leavened, the tree would grow, and the birds of the air would come and lodge in its branches.

Over time I would come to understand much about the very specific real-world ways in which all these things would come about. This would include understanding how the lion would lie down with the lamb, and who the little child is that would lead them.

Angela and I made the decision to declare ourselves Bahá'ís at the same time. There was an event at the Bahá'í Center in Los Angeles, and we met there with the Local Spiritual Assembly to discuss and announce our decision. We hadn't really noticed that the date was May 23. The event was the anniversary of the declaration of the Báb.

It might be fair to ask about the Sign of the Bahá'í covenant.

Earlier I referenced the first Hidden Word, about possessing a pure heart. The second Hidden Word says that justice is Bahá'u'lláh's gift to us and the sign of His lovingkindness.[6] But it also says that everyone must see it through his or her own eyes. I wonder if perhaps the Sign of His covenant is a unique Sign for each of us. If my hypothesis is correct, we represent an infinite number of parallel universes, brought together not by external forces but by voluntary movement—free radicals deciding to begin the process of circumambulation.

Whether this was true or not, when Angela and I were asked to speak at the celebration of the declaration of the Báb, I knew what to say. I shared with the

---

6 Bahá'u'lláh - The Hidden Words, Arabic no. 2.

audience that I had been in a ten-year dedicated search for those who fulfilled the Sign of the Christian covenant—those who loved one another. And that God had shown me that my audience was composed of those people.

Writing this now brings tears to my eyes, mostly because several people in the audience told me that what I had said had brought tears to theirs. And yet the day of our declaration was only the beginning of a process. That process was not without its initial challenges for me.

IT DON'T COME EASY

I soon entered a tailspin with the young founders I had joined to launch Gohuman.com. Certainly, it had to do with a lack of success and the fact that I was beginning to doubt we could be successful. But that wasn't what led to an unraveling, and it's hard to say exactly what the primary reason for it was. The best I can do is to put it down to a generation gap.

I was much older, was the only one married, and the other founders' solution to the problems we faced was to express their willingness to live in a garage and work 24/7 until the company became profitable—without a clear plan on what would enable profitability. And, on the flip side, they were perhaps having challenges dealing with my relatively immature efforts to attain the amazingly high Bahá'í standard of treating each and every individual with love and respect. While I was an adult in the school of life and business, I was a baby Bahá'í who didn't realize the power of kindness and respect, or the debilitating effects on others when it wasn't there.

As my three young cofounders and I began to disagree on the path forward, the admittedly meager momentum we were building came to a screeching halt. I reacted by becoming more vocal and insistent, to which they eventually reacted by calling for a vote on having me step back from all my responsibilities. Having been outvoted three-to-one, I politely stepped back and watched from a distance as the potential of the company I had cofounded was vaporized by the lack of a clear or realistic vision and the experience needed to grow a real-world business.

Having stepped away from the corporate world, I felt like I had lost my professional momentum, along with a significant portion of what my new wife and I might have otherwise classified as a nest egg.

Whether we would have the financial means needed or not, in October 2007 it became official. There was an egg in our nest. After having tried for eight years in my previous marriage, I was skeptical that I would ever have children, so this came as an unexpected surprise to both of us. Angela was less excited, but I was ecstatic. Of all the monumental changes I had gone through, the miracle of being part of creating a new life was by far one of the most humbling.

As I waited, with only a small measure of hope, to see if my partners could pull off a glove save of GoHuman.com, I scrambled to finish my MBA and worked diligently to find a new professional orbit as quickly as possible. It hadn't really dawned on me just how much the arrival of a child would change my life, but a serious fire had been lit under my backside, nonetheless.

Pregnancy is a mother-daughter bonding event that inevitably leads to the inevitable. In biological terms, Dad locates the branch, gathers twigs, and buys designer baby furniture for the nest Mom instinctively wants, wherever Mom instinctively wants it. Mom instinctively wants to be closer to her mother, which overrides the allure of the balmy temperatures of Southern California. So, in December I found myself in Madison, Wisconsin, interviewing with CUNA Mutual Group for a position to build an IT vendor management function.

CUNA Mutual wasn't the first company I interviewed with in the Milwaukee/Madison area, but it was the one I was most excited about. I refer to them as "the backbone of the credit union movement." If you can imagine what the corporate headquarters of big banks like Bank of America (which ended up acquiring Countrywide, still flying very high in 2007) or Wells Fargo Bank (which had then recently gobbled up Washington Mutual) are like, then you can imagine CUNA Mutual. All the small local and regional credit unions across the US and, to a degree, Canada, function as its bank branches.

CUNA Mutual supports these local and regional credit unions with products and services, such as insurance, credit cards, and much more. I quickly realized that this represented an alternative to the massive financial institutions I had worked for at Deloitte and Countrywide. Credit unions are small, locally owned, not-for-profit financial institutions. Even before "too big to fail" became a household phrase, I recognized these credit unions as the solution, a viable alternative to the global finance system. I wanted in.

Having learned about Babylon the Great from the inside of corporate America and having caught the bug of wanting to do something about it from being a cofounder of GoHuman.com, I realized CUNA Mutual was exactly what I needed. I gave the interview process my best, and then waited anxiously for an answer.

CUNA Mutual, it turned out, wanted me too. And they were savvy enough to deliver an offer to me over Christmas, while we were visiting my in-laws.

CUNA Mutual expected my in-laws to apply pressure for me to accept. And they did.

The pressure wasn't necessary, as I wanted nothing more than to accept the position, which came with a juicy relocation package. After all, the economy was still booming—and the bubble had not yet imploded. With my background and a bit of divine backing, who knows what might happen. From within that world, I might even find a way to make GoHuman.com work.

I agreed to start work in Madison in cold, dark January, while Angela stayed in sunny Southern California until April.

A few days later, back in Pasadena, Angela and I were out in "chilly" but sunny sixty-degree weather on New Year's Day, 2008. We were watching flower-covered floats and miniskirted baton twirlers proclaim the beauty of the sun and its ability to produce roses. The Rose Parade route begins on Orange Grove Boulevard, and Angela had treated a couple of the residents on this prestigious stretch of real estate through her physical therapy practice. Bleachers had been set up on their lawn, and we were invited to the party.

Across the street was Ambassador College, where twenty-eight years prior, almost to the day, I had arrived from Alaska to embark on an amazing study into the Word of God.

Very eccentric and irregular orbits had brought me right back to the point where my exploration had begun in earnest.

This was ground zero of my spiritual odyssey, the launching pad of a frantic search that had taken me around the world looking for God.

Eventually, this search had led me to the moon, which I had been following for most of my life, and back.

Before the next full moon, I'd be leaving Pasadena. Like my father before me, who had sought to point me in the right direction, I would be focused on the same for my family, on our orbit through space-time.

We might be heading for colder climates, but since the light is constant, and since it approaches us at the same speed, no matter which direction we might travel in, or how fast or how slow we might be traveling, whatever source of light might reach us, we would be turning toward it.

And there would be no turning back.

APPENDIX 1

The Moon

I think I should tell you, something you already know
You're with me on this journey
I think about you, wherever I go
I'm hoping that you had a good night
I'm hoping that your dreams give you flight
I'm hoping that this day turns out right

I'm hoping that you had a good night
I'm hoping that this day turns out right
I'm hoping soon to see the sight

Of your beautiful face
Amazing Grace
Give me the time
Name any place
And I'll be by your side

'Coz you are the moon
And I am the tide

APPENDIX 2

Isaiah 58

New King James Version (NKJV)

58 "Cry aloud, spare not; lift up your voice like a trumpet;

Tell My people their transgression, and the house of Jacob their sins.

2 Yet they seek Me daily, and delight to know My ways, as a nation that did righteousness, and did not forsake the ordinance of their God.

They ask of Me the ordinances of justice; they take delight in approaching God.

3 'Why have we fasted,' they say, 'and You have not seen?

Why have we afflicted our souls, and You take no notice?'

"In fact, in the day of your fast you find pleasure, and exploit all your laborers.

4 Indeed you fast for strife and debate, and to strike with the fist of wickedness.

You will not fast as you do this day, to make your voice heard on high.

5 Is it a fast that I have chosen, a day for a man to afflict his soul?

Is it to bow down his head like a bulrush, and to spread out sackcloth and ashes?

Would you call this a fast, and an acceptable day to the Lord?

6 "Is this not the fast that I have chosen:

To loose the bonds of wickedness, to undo the heavy burdens, to let the oppressed go free, and that you break every yoke?

7 Is it not to share your bread with the hungry, and that you bring to your house the poor who are cast out; when you see the naked, that you cover him, and not hide yourself from your own flesh?

8 Then your light shall break forth like the morning, your healing shall spring forth speedily,

And your righteousness shall go before you; the glory of the LORD shall be your rear guard.

9 Then you shall call, and the LORD will answer; you shall cry, and He will say, 'Here I am.'

"If you take away the yoke from your midst, the pointing of the finger, and speaking wickedness,

10 If you extend your soul to the hungry and satisfy the afflicted soul, then your light shall dawn in the darkness, and your darkness shall be as the noonday.

11 The LORD will guide you continually, and satisfy your soul in drought, and strengthen your bones; you shall be like a watered garden, and like a spring of water, whose waters do not fail.

12 Those from among you shall build the old waste places; you shall raise up the foundations of many generations; and you shall be called the Repairer of the Breach, the Restorer of Streets to Dwell In.

13 "If you turn away your foot from the Sabbath, from doing your pleasure on My holy day, and call the Sabbath a delight, the holy day of the LORD honorable, and shall honor Him, not doing your own ways, nor finding your own pleasure, nor speaking your own words,

14 Then you shall delight yourself in the LORD; and I will cause you to ride on the high hills of the earth, and feed you with the heritage of Jacob your father.

The mouth of the LORD has spoken."

APPENDIX 3

The Báb's Letter to the Living

The Báb - The Herald of the Day of Days:

O My beloved friends! You are the bearers of the name of God in this Day.
You have been chosen as the repositories of His mystery.
It behooves each one of you to manifest the attributes of

God, and to exemplify by your deed and words the signs of His righteousness,
His power and glory. The very members of your body must bear witness to the
loftiness of your purpose, the integrity of your life, the reality of your faith, and
the exalted character of your devotion. For verily I say, this is the Day spoken of
by God in His Book: 'On that day will We set a seal upon their mouths; yet shall
their hands speak unto Us, and their feet shall bear witness to that which they
shall have done.'

Ponder the words of Jesus addressed to His disciples, as He sent them forth
to propagate the Cause of God. In words such as these, He bade them arise and
fulfill their mission: 'Ye are even as the fire which in the darkness of the night has
been kindled upon the mountain-top. Let your light shine before the eyes of men.
Such must be the purity of your character and the degree of your renunciation
that the people of the earth may through you recognize and be drawn closer to
the heavenly Father who is the Source of purity and grace. For none has seen the
Father who is in heaven. You who are His spiritual children must by your deeds
exemplify His virtues, and witness to His glory. You are the salt of the earth, but if
the salt have lost its savor, wherewith shall it be salted?

'Such must be the degree of your detachment, that into whatever city you enter to proclaim and teach the Cause of God, you should in no wise expect either meat or reward from its people. Nay, when you depart out of that city, you should shake the dust from off your feet. As you have entered it pure and undefiled, so must you depart from that city. For verily I say, the heavenly Father is ever with you and keeps watch over you. If you be faithful to Him, He will assuredly deliver into your hands all the treasures of the earth, and will exalt you above all the rulers and kings of the world.'

O My Letters! Verily I say, immensely exalted is this Day above the days of the Apostles of old. Nay, immeasurable is the difference. You are the witnesses of the Dawn of the promised Day of God. You are the partakers of the mystic chalice of His Revelation. Gird up the loins of endeavor, and be mindful of the words of God as revealed in His Book: 'Lo the Lord thy God is come, and with Him is the company of His angels arrayed before Him!'

Purge your hearts of worldly desires, and let angelic virtues be your adorning. Strive that by your deeds you may bear witness to the truth of these words of God, and beware lest, by 'turning back,' He may 'change you for another people,' who 'shall not be your like,' and who shall take from you the Kingdom of God.

The days when idle worship was deemed sufficient are ended. The time is come when naught but the purest motive, supported by deeds of stainless purity, can ascend to the throne of the Most High and be acceptable unto Him.

—(H. M. Balyuzi, *The Báb - The Herald of the Day of Days*,
George Ronald, publisher, 1973, p. 29)